Results at the Top

BARBARA ANNIS | RICHARD NESBITT

Results at the Top

USING **GENDER INTELLIGENCE**
TO CREATE
BREAKTHROUGH GROWTH

WILEY

Published by John Wiley & Sons, Inc., Hoboken, New Jersey
Published simultaneously in Canada

For general information about our other products and services, please contact our Customer Care Department within the United States at (800) 762-2974, outside the United States at (317) 572-3993 or fax (317) 572-4002.

Wiley publishes in a variety of print and electronic formats and by print-on-demand. Some material included with standard print versions of this book may not be included in e-books or in print-on-demand. If this book refers to media such as a CD or DVD that is not included in the version you purchased, you may download this material at http://booksupport.wiley.com. For more information about Wiley products, visit www.wiley.com.

Library of Congress Cataloging-in-Publication Data is Available:

ISBN 978-1-119-38408-3 (Hardcover)
ISBN 978-1-119-38402-1 (ePDF)
ISBN 978-1-119-38407-6 (ePub)

Cover Design: Wiley
Cover Image: © peshkov/Getty Images

Printed in the United States of America

10 9 8 7 6 5 4 3 2 1

Barbara Annis:

To my husband, Paul Reed Currie, whose amazing support, love, and integrity I always admire and treasure. And to my wonderful children, Lauren, Sasha, Stéphane, and Christian; my bonus children, Zachary, Kelly, and Jeremy; and my grandchildren, Colin, Cameron, Alaia, Brydan, Jake, Riley, and Grayson.

Richard Nesbitt:

It is with deep gratitude and the utmost appreciation that I dedicate this book to the many courageous and honorable women and men whom I have had the privilege of working, learning, and growing with throughout my career. Their knowledge, integrity, and perseverance have taught me so much for which I am eternally grateful. I would like to thank my co-author Barbara Annis, who I have known, worked with, and respected for over two decades, for helping us achieve our vision of creating a book that speaks to men and women.

I am exceedingly thankful to my parents, siblings, grandparents, aunts, and uncles for their many sage and critical life lessons taught to me during my developing years on the farm.

I dedicate this book to my exceptional daughters, Olivia and Lillian, who continue to educate and inspire me each day with their wisdom and joie de vivre. You are both a constant source of joy, wonder, pride, and inspiration.

And I am most grateful to my wife and biggest fan, Lucy, my trusted advisor and life partner of more than thirty-four years. Her encouragement, suggestions, guidance, and enthusiasm have kept me motivated and encouraged throughout the writing of this book.

CONTENTS

ACKNOWLEDGMENTS

We would like to thank John Fayad, our senior editor for *Results at the Top*. This book is only possible through his diligent efforts and valuable advice over many months. He is a true advocate for inclusion and diversity who is making it happen in business every day.

BARBARA ANNIS

I wish to acknowledge the many men and women with whom I have worked closely over the years for their deep commitment to creating a more gender-intelligent world for us, for our children, and for each succeeding generation.

My deepest appreciation to the women leaders and staff at the Women's Leadership Board, Harvard Kennedy School. I am honored to partner with you in your commitment to creating a world where men and women are equally valued and respected in all aspects of economic, political, and social life.

I also wish to recognize the thousands of men and women whom I have met over the years, at all levels of leadership across the globe, who want nothing more than to find ways to work together more inclusively and productively and to find greater success and satisfaction in their careers and in their personal lives.

Finally, I must recognize the organizations, both past and present, with which I have worked so closely for their amazing, dedicated men and women in positions of leadership creating cultures of Gender Intelligence.

RICHARD NESBITT

My thanks go out to those who read earlier drafts of this book and provided their valuable comments. I would also like to thank my fellow professors at Rotman who gave me advice and helped me head in the right direction. In particular, I would like to thank Tiff Macklem, dean of the Rotman School of Management, and Mihnea Moldoveanu, vice dean, Rotman School of Management, for their support and guidance.

Important parts of my education in diversity have come from my work with Women in Capital Markets. This organization continues to do tremendous work in improving our financial markets through greater inclusion.

I would also like to thank my assistant, Bernadette Fernandes, who has supported me for many years in my various projects, including *Results at the Top*.

My gratitude to all of the contributors, who are too numerous to name. They have provided their stories from their real-world experience for inclusion in our book. From them we are able to learn about what works and what doesn't work. They are role models for all of us who seek to improve our organizations. Speaking of role models, I wish to acknowledge the visionary male leaders who have recognized the economic power of men and women leading together, and who are actively involved in advancing women in leadership.

INTRODUCTION

For decades, the burden for achieving parity in leadership, whether in business, education, or government, has been placed squarely, and wrongly, on the shoulders of women alone. There are few if any books written *specifically* to men on gender diversity and what men can and should do to support and champion the advancement of women into leadership roles.

Nevertheless, we see an entirely different phenomenon that's taking place today and coming at us at a high rate of speed. We see an expanding realization on the part of men—in pockets all over the globe—that sharing leadership with women produces superior performance in organizations. Virtually every financial study conducted since the 1980s on the financial performance of companies that have women on their boards and their executive teams have proven it to be true!

Male leaders know the value. What they don't know is how to engage and be supportive in advancing women. *Results at the Top* is the first book of its kind written primarily—though not exclusively—for men, showing them exactly why organizational performance is better and how to get on board.

Results at the Top will be of high interest to women as well, for by speaking to men and making known their thoughts and the reasons for their behaviors, we reveal to women how to best communicate and interact with men in the workplace, and in many other aspects of life.

We're embarking on a new level of achievement in the pursuit of women in leadership, and this book is recognition of that achievement and points directly to the successes gained.

Our title, *Results at the Top*, speaks to that success and the intersection of the three transformational events happening in countries across the globe that are bringing about that acknowledgment and success. These events are culminating in the rise of companies' Gender Intelligence quotient, shareholder value, and the broader measures of superior corporate performance.

- *The ascent of neuroscience* and our expanding awareness of the distinct yet complementary natures of men and women
- *The ascent of women* in dominating education and moving into positions of leadership
- *The ascent of men* in their recognition of and advocacy for women in leadership

This book fixes its sights on these three elements, with particular focus on the ascent of men, and spotlights trends in their attitudes and behaviors as well as their successes in advancing women in the organizations that they lead. It's also a book in which men can discover more about themselves, how they tick, and why. Unlike so many books and articles written about men, we are *not* here to place blame, but to understand men's strengths and contributions and how they differ from those of women.

Nor do we address issues such as how women should conduct themselves to be most effective in today's companies. Previous books on this and related topics are plentiful and are usually addressed only to women, or to some vague blend of men and women.

Today, women equal or outnumber men in universities, law schools, and medical schools, and for the first time in the United States, in 2009 women received a greater percentage of doctorate degrees. They've represented nearly half the workforce since the 1980s and influence almost 80 percent of consumer purchases globally. They are joining the ranks of business entrepreneurs in increasing numbers—on average, running more financially successful small businesses than their male entrepreneur counterparts.

But there is one outpost where women are a distinct minority, and not by their own choice—in the senior leadership teams and boards of public corporations. Despite the acclaim given to a few high-profile female CEOs, around 90 percent of companies today are still led by men.

The discrepancy has not gone unnoticed. Gender diversity is one of the hottest topics in business today. Why are women not advancing at the pace they would like? Why do regulators feel it necessary to mandate gender diversity in public companies? Why, after forty years of mandates, are women still only one out of five on executive teams and one out of ten as CEOs?

Results at the Top brings to business leaders—male leaders—a "dollars and cents" rationale and proven reasons to change their attitudes. Our book delivers proof of a virtually universal relationship between the presence of women on boards and in senior management teams and improved corporate performance. And it proposes a series of concrete steps that corporations can and should take to promote greater gender diversity at each stage of the career ladder.

We offer groundbreaking insights into what will motivate companies to hire more women into senior management and appoint them to more board positions. We examine the relationship between the number of women on a board of a company and the number of women on the top management team of that company, advancing a new method of evaluating diversity in a company's leadership called the Gender Propensity Index©, or GPI©.

Do a company's policies and leadership behaviors indicate the likelihood of new women being added to management and boards? Will this lead to superior performance? Many stakeholders want to know the answers to these questions, from the companies themselves to their employees, their new hires, and their shareholders. It will also be of interest to regulators and other government agencies.

Results at the Top discusses how men should respond to these challenges and how men and women can work together to achieve the common goal of running better organizations. We address the importance of measurement and action to realize enhanced performance through gender diversity and how organizations should rid their "plumbing" of bias as a first and most critical step.

We're on the crest of this tidal wave and beginning to see the effects of gender-balanced leadership on the productivity and financial performance of companies. In time, this wave will carry over onto the global economy and into governments around the world.

Countries are beginning to realize and embrace, as equals, their greatest undervalued and underdeveloped economic resource—the female half of the population. We believe the engagement of women in developing countries for their balanced voice in business and government will be one of the greatest breakthroughs for humankind in the twenty-first century.

The solution right under our noses is in bringing the best brains of both men and women together to create a better, more stable world—both economically and socially. Imagine how different our world would be right now if women had been at the table just in the last fifty years.

Our hope is that, with our book, we can encourage and influence just 10 percent of the male leadership in companies around the world and accelerate the progress that's already been made. Our hope is that *Results at the Top* will be a wake-up call for more men to get on board and give rise to an even more powerful movement forward.

We believe that if we can get this right, we could achieve real progress in a single generation.

Chapter 1

YOUR WAKE-UP CALL

Let's put it on the table right at the onset. We believe—and what's more, we believe we can prove—that if you want your business to perform at its peak, you must hire and promote women alongside men into management and elect them to your board of directors.

How we can possibly be doing the best for our businesses if we hire and promote from only one-half of the population? This question has been out there forever, including back when women were not even considered full citizens. Asking this question has not led to the experience that most women and many men want, which is a full place for women alongside men in management and on boards. Other authors have tried to argue that women have superior skills (at least in certain areas) and this is the reason they should succeed in business. How is that argument working for change? Not so well.

We need to make a case that is provable based on evidence from an overwhelming number of experts in the field—a case that matters to those in positions of power. Who are they? Why—men, of course. This is the challenge that many who have tried to create change have been unable to resolve.

DIVERSITY AT THE TOP: CORRELATES WITH BETTER PERFORMANCE

For over twenty years, a growing body of research has demonstrated that companies that embrace diversity in general—and gender diversity at the highest company levels in particular—enjoy superior corporate performance. The evidence is globally relevant. It applies as much to China as to the United States and as much to Canada as to the United Kingdom or any other country.

Acting to achieve optimal corporate performance, or as some statutes require, "acting in the best interests of the corporation," requires boards and management to adjust the balance in their firm to achieve the right mix of men and women in leadership roles.

However, some believe progress by corporations in this area has stalled of late. Despite the acclaim given to a few high-profile female CEOs, progress in promoting women to senior management roles has slowed in mature economies. Writing recently in *The New York Times*, Philip N. Cohen noted that, "The movement toward equality stopped [in 1994] and it hasn't changed much since."[1]

Men still dominate senior management and boards, with women representing a little more than a token presence. There is no question that women feel "left out" and frustrated, as is suggested by the title of a *Harvard Business Review* article, "Women in Management: Delusion of Progress."[2]

However, if you consider that the aim is a fundamental change in the way men and women interact with each other at work, we can see progress continuing globally with distinct regional dynamics.

That's the bottom line of our book. And unlike other books written today on the topic of advancing women, this is not another "your journey to diversity" book. We're offering more than that. We know what works and we're going to show you how to do it. We're going to share breakthrough insights, pinpoint the specific areas where you need to focus your attention, and give you the tools to make things happen.

This book is unique in another way as well. There are few if any books on gender diversity targeted *specifically* to men and what men can and should do to support and champion the advancement of women. For decades, the burden for achieving parity in leadership, whether in business, education, or government, has been placed squarely, and wrongly, on the shoulders of women alone.

That's changing. We see a growing realization on the part of male leaders all over the globe that women in balanced leadership with men leads to a bigger bottom line. These leaders are personally getting involved and seeing that their managers at all levels are walking the talk as well.

Men in positions of power want to see more women on their executive teams and on their boards. Many confess, though, that they don't know what to do to make that happen. Many admit that they didn't know that they *personally* needed to be involved. They also admitted that they are seldom if ever invited to participate in gender diversity programs. But when we share with them the contents of this book, they're totally receptive, supportive, and enthusiastic about getting involved.

Men, you are the last piece of the puzzle in this quest for the advancement of women, and this is your one-of-a-kind guidebook in how to get personally involved and what specifically you can do.

Women, you will find *Results at the Top* of huge value as well for its refreshingly different insights into why men on executive teams and boards—well, men in general — think and act as they do. You're going to learn a lot about yourselves as well in the chapters that follow.

Most important, it will help women leaders in Human Resources and Diversity & Inclusion to know where and how we're suggesting men get involved. You may not be aware of the critical mass of men who want to be partners in this. So, we're inviting you to invite them!

> "Speaking of being partners in this, Richard, we've both been at this for quite a few years now. Let's tell our readers what first brought us together."
>
> "I remember it well, Barbara. I was working inside, in banking, trying to effect change, while you were working outside, bringing Gender Intelligence to all kinds of industries everywhere."

HOW WE CAME TOGETHER

I first met Barbara in 1990 when she was asked by John Hunkin, then Chairman and CEO of the Canadian Imperial Bank of Commerce (CIBC), to come in and improve the working culture of CIBC and Wood Gundy, the retail brokerage division of CIBC Wealth Management.

At that time, I was the senior manager in fixed income; I then moved to the equity division. It was that position in equity that opened my eyes to the company's maternity policy, something I initially tried to ignore. I'll explain that a little later on in this chapter.

Richard Venn was one of the first men I ever knew who championed women in leadership. At the time, he was president of CIBC/Wood Gundy. Richard was directly involved in bringing Barbara and her Gender Intelligence workshops into the organization. I attended a number of sessions and remember them well. The business case and brain science opened my eyes to the value of difference thinking. Since then, Barbara and I have stayed in touch and tracked each other's work for twenty years.

I remember Barbara facilitating the Gender Intelligence workshops with Wood Gundy. That firm was way ahead of the curve when it came to recognizing the value and need to have women in retail brokerage and in leadership. Wood Gundy was one of the first banks to tackle this issue and transform the trading floor culture.

More companies today are discovering that in order to achieve superior performance, they'll need the critical thinking skills of both men and women on the board level, on the executive committee, and on every management team right down through to the market-facing consultants, advisers, and sales teams.

> "You know, Richard, your recollection of when we first met takes me a little further back in my career and how I came to realize the necessity of engaging men in the advancement of women."

BARBARA'S WAKE-UP CALL

The time was the early 1980s and the place was the multinational firm Sony. I was climbing the corporate ladder, well on my way to becoming Sony's first female sales manager. It had been a tough journey, but I made it to the top and raised three children at the same time. I felt like I had scored a great victory for women. I was sure my story would inspire working women everywhere. And I was sure I knew the formula for success: you had to behave like a man.

Life at Sony was hectic, tough, and competitive. To tackle all the obstacles in my way, I attended—literally—a hundred coaching sessions on topics ranging from *Assertiveness Training* to *Guerrilla War Tactics for Women*. The sessions were more like military training camps than anything, but I kept going to them. Why? They worked! I won more outstanding performance awards than any of my colleagues did. I became such a tough manager that some of my colleagues nicknamed me "The Sherman Tank."

Like many working women at the time, I believed that to be *equal* to men women had to be *the same* as men. Actually, back in the 1970s and 1980s, many feminists believed women had to be the same but better—women had to study more, work harder, and perform better than men to succeed. Basically, everyone thought the only model for success was the male model.

Nobody thought much about gender differences back then. Like everyone else, I thought "inferior to men" meant "less than men." I bought into that thinking. I was a split personality: a man in the office, and a woman in my personal relationships and with my clients. I actually bought into the *same is equal* thinking so much that I decided to help other women learn to act more like men too. After all, it was the way to success.

When I looked around, I saw a lot of women struggling to make it in the corporate world, but not that many actually running companies or sitting in boardrooms. I was sure it was because women weren't trying hard enough. I believed women were self-defeating and took things too personally, or just failed to make themselves heard. I told women to get off it and stop being drama queens. That's what the men said—and I bought into it. I told women they had to become powerful, authoritative, and assertive, and suppress their emotions and talk like a boss. It worked for me!

I stuck to this crusade for several years until one fateful incident at a workshop I was giving for women at the pharmaceutical company SmithKline Beecham. When I look back now, I can see how that workshop turned my whole world-view upside down and led me to do the work I do today.

The workshop had started the usual way, with me preaching on about how women had to take control of their lives. When I got to the part about how to gain respect from your boss, one woman in the group stopped me.

"Why are you saying that it's women who have to change?" she asked. "What about men?"

In my mind, different meant less. There was a hierarchy, and women were lower on the ladder. I told the woman, "If you're here, it's because you're missing something."

She didn't buy it. "We're not here because we think something's wrong with us. The problem is in the work environment. It is devaluing. That's all."

I stuck to my line. "If you feel devalued, maybe there's something wrong with the way you put yourself across."

But the woman didn't buy that either, and neither did any of her colleagues at the workshop. Exasperated, I ended the workshop and sent them home. I also went home—to think. And that's when I began to see that I had been getting it all wrong, all along. I understood that there was no point trying to make women act like men. Women were different from men!

At the time, I was also giving workshops to men on how to relate to women. The men actually acted very differently in workshops than women did. The men didn't nod while I was speaking, like the women. They didn't collaborate or brainstorm the same way as women. They didn't draw up lists the same way or discuss things the same way either. When I thought about my work at Sony, I realized that men and women worked differently there, too. I had always chalked these differences up to personality differences, but I started wondering if there wasn't more to it.

Well, there was! I decided to see what scientists and researchers were saying about gender differences and they had a lot to say! By the mid-1980s, the facts were there. Men and women really were different. They think differently. They process information differently. They communicate differently.

What a huge mistake it has been, and continues to be, to try to turn women into men! Ever since that fateful workshop at the pharmaceutical company, my life has been dedicated to showing men and women how they are different, and helping them overcome the challenges caused by their differences. And we can see change happening today.

"That's a great story, Barbara. You found a way to succeed at Sony by accepting the environment and changing your nature to fit in. You just assumed, as many women and men do today, that the business environment is what it is and that you either learn to swim or drown. Men across the globe are now realizing that it's the environment that needs to change, not the women in it."

"You have your own story, Richard. You saw through that blind spot years ago, around the time when we first met at CIBC Wood Gundy."

"That's right, Barbara. Over the run of my career, I've learned that including women and men in my management teams led to superior results compared to men alone (or women alone, although that rarely happened). I didn't come to this conclusion until I had substantial experience in management."

WHEN I BECAME A REAL MANAGER OF PEOPLE

The truth is, I didn't care much about the issue of advancing women in management and leadership for the first half of my working life. What I really cared about was my own advancement. But as I took on larger, more complex tasks, I had to seek greater diversity in the creation of the teams. Inevitably I became convinced that diversity led to better results than if I had limited myself to the narrower universe of men. I didn't really know why this happened, but just accepted it as fact.

I became an advocate for this approach in the firms that I joined. My views often met with mixed reactions, but I didn't care. It worked for me, and I intended to keep doing it. As I became more senior, I was able to effect systemic change in the firms I served. We would hire more women graduates at the introductory level, we would have programs to hang on to these women through the critical first seven to ten years of their career, and we would move women into more senior levels to be visible role models not only to other women but also to men.

In order to build support for this approach I had to get the men I worked with on my side. Remember: today, it is men who lead most companies—which is why this book speaks to men about how it is in their interest to change their preconceptions and behavior.

The first task is to drop as much gender bias as possible from what I call the "plumbing" of the company, a concept Barbara and I will explore more closely in a later chapter.

This meant recruitment committees had to be balanced. Promotion committees had to be balanced, not just in terms of numbers but also in terms of power. Getting the plumbing right meant changing our hiring practices and setting targets that would help us achieve our goals. It also meant changing benefit policies to accept that good maternity leave policies see more women returning from maternity leave. It meant ensuring that we were considering women as well as men in everything we did, from interviews to succession planning and board appointments.

My employer's maternity leave policies were probably the last thing on my mind in my first five years as an employee without management responsibilities. As a male employee, what possible interest could I have in these policies? Surely people wiser and more experienced than I had adopted policies at some time in the past that were fair and reasonable to both the employee and the firm.

Once I moved into management, I remember a friend outside the equity division telling me that some people were unhappy with my leadership. I couldn't understand why, given that our financial results had dramatically improved under my leadership. What more could I do for the company and for the employees? My friend told me some employees felt that I was insensitive to their needs and were, at the least, calling my leadership into question. It seemed to center around the maternity issue.

About the same time, Richard Venn, president of Wood Gundy, asked me to come see him. I assumed that I was going to be commended for the equities division's financial performance. To my surprise, it was to discuss my role with regard to the division's maternity policies.

Richard Venn listened to me as I explained that I assumed that the company had good policies and the whole matter was someone else's responsibility. Richard said that was not good enough, that I was their leader, and they expected me to act for them. He clearly wanted me to do something and that was fine by me. I knew I would have his support.

After reflecting on it that evening I decided to go to the source and sit down with some of the employees who were being affected and find out what was bothering them. It didn't take long for these discussions to get right to the point. The point was that our maternity policies were unfair and uncompetitive and what was I going to do about it? They saw me as their boss and their only hope to effect change.

My next step was to find out why our policies were unfair and uncompetitive. Of course this was not the prevailing view of the HR department, and so, with that department's help, I began an analysis of maternity policies at other leading firms. It became clear to me that we were on the lower end of the quality spectrum.

This was not good enough. Given that we were a leading firm, this didn't seem to fit with our position in the industry. I decided that we should have the best maternity policies in the industry, commensurate with our position as a market leader. I would institute these new maternity policies for the women who worked for me in capital markets. Then the rest of the firm would follow, and they did!

> "I credit you, Barbara, for my education back then. In my experience, there are diversity programs that work, but many simply don't work. Yet, companies roll them out year after year with the standard assigned quotas and metrics. Everyone wants to do the right thing, but those decades-old initiatives just haven't moved the needle."
>
> "That is so true, Richard. And what we've discovered over the years is that, in virtually every instance, the differentiating factor between failure and success is whether male leaders are all in and involved. Let me explain what I mean."

THE DIVERSITY MONEY PIT

We recently conducted a study to assess the diversity programs that created a sustainable impact in advancing women into senior management. We gathered data from three technology companies, four financial services firms, and two accounting firms.[3] We'll first outline the perennial diversity programs that have shown minimal success and explain why. We'll then highlight the programs that are working well and helping to move women into leadership positions.

We all know what a money pit is—an ongoing drain on financial resources. With all the best of intentions, and implemented by great people dedicated to effecting change, here are the top diversity programs that the companies in the study admit have not produced the desired results. Richard and I will explain these in more detail in later chapters.

Women's Networks

Women's networks, councils, and chapters that lacked strategy and linkage to the financial objectives of the company ended up becoming no more than social networks. Meetings often became a venue for voicing complaints, but not linked to any initiatives in order to drive positive change. Many women said that the networks increased their sense of separateness from the rest of the organization.

It's still happening today. Whenever women's councils or networks invite us to give a keynote or seminar on how women can advance in their leadership and careers, we ask what percentage of the audience will be male.

It's almost as if we're speaking a different language. It either doesn't dawn on these groups that male leaders and influencers need to be involved or that they would even be interested in women's career issues. Some confess that they really don't know how to go about getting men to participate.

Training for Women

Training for women tended to place the onus on "fixing" women. Many of the companies' management and leadership development programs were initially designed for their male leaders and were now being used to define women's leadership and essentially help them fit into a sameness model—instead of mining for their own unique leadership styles.

Focus on the Numbers

Many companies assumed that critical mass through quotas was the answer—that it was just a matter of stepping up their annual recruitment efforts. The problems they were having with the retention of women hires were assumed to be bad fits or women leaving for work-life reasons.

Millions are spent each year on recruiting more women into companies at the entry level and on hiring them directly into senior management roles. The reality is that over the past forty years, women have done no better than to represent 22 percent of senior management, which has changed very little in the past ten years, and less that 5 percent of CEO positions.[4]

Work-Life Flexibility Policies

These programs are a great value to many women, especially at the entry and mid-management level. The companies in the study used work-life flexibility programs as an engagement strategy to bring young women into a company, but they had little to no impact on advancing women to senior positions.

You'll discover that even in countries that legislate that companies must comply with work-life flexibility policies, women's representation in senior management is no better than the global average.

Women's Mentors

There were a few flaws that surfaced in mentoring programs. Companies found that their mentors, both women and men, were not trained on the differences that often arise when mentoring women and men.

Moreover, women mentees were matched with women mentors instead of being matched with men. Aside from there not being enough women in leadership to mentor the number of women mentees, in many instances, women-to-women matches didn't have the right chemistry and failed.

Diversity Workshops

Diversity and compliance training for men generally created a reverse effect. Men were trained to ignore gender differences and treat everyone the same. They became overly sensitive, politically correct, and afraid to acknowledge any gender differences.

Male executives often confide in us that out of fear of unconsciously saying or doing something wrong or insensitive, they will become cautious and brief in their discussions with women; many have difficulty giving critical feedback to women on their teams; and some even admit that they avoid interactions with women, especially in informal settings.

In Chapter 2, you're going to see some interesting statistics on the number of sex-discrimination charges filed with the Equal Employment Opportunity Commission in the United States over the past eighteen years. It seems that diversity-training programs, including unconscious bias training, which began around twenty years ago, are not having the desired effect. We answer the question: "Why?"

WHAT MAKES THE DIFFERENCE

We expect that our observations and recommendations will challenge some men and women. We know the reaction in some cases will be, "You cannot say that," or "You cannot make that generalization." But the topics we are going to discuss are things we have observed time and time again that explain why men still dominate today's corporations despite forty years of diversity efforts in trying to affect otherwise.

We reveal why many gender diversity programs, with all the best of intentions, are doing little to nothing to change company cultures to be more inclusive and improve the gender equation. Some companies we know spend tens of millions of dollars a year on women's initiatives, with negligible change in women's representation in the senior ranks.

"I believe, Barbara, that our describing the Diversity Money Pit programs will for sure challenge some readers. Those who develop and manage those diversity programs annually have the best of intentions; but with so little success to show year after year, I sometimes wonder, who are the beneficiaries of those best intentions? Let me explain what I mean."

BRUSHING YOUR HORSE

I have always enjoyed working with horses. Since I was a child I spent summers at my grandparents' farm and I have always been around horses. Horses are large animals and you need to give them respect when you are near them. They have many ways to (sometimes intentionally but mostly unintentionally) deliver you a bruise that you will remember for a long time. So what has this got to do with improving corporate performance?

I remember one day we were putting my horse away after having been out for a ride. You normally hang up the tack, inspect and clean the horse's feet, and make sure that the horse is in a good condition. I remember saying to my uncle who was watching me and who taught me most of the things I knew about caring for my pony, "Do you think my horse might like it if I brushed him?" My uncle replied, "I don't know whether the horse really cares but you would probably enjoy it."

At the time I did not think much about his comment, as I was eight years old. So I brushed my horse and felt really good that he looked well groomed. Of course, the moment we let the horse go into the paddock field he found a nice dusty spot and proceeded to roll around in it, undoing all of my fancy brushing work.

This comment stayed with me for the rest of my life. Why did my uncle say that? Perhaps he meant that I should go ahead and spend my time and effort on something that felt good to me. The fact that no one else (including my horse!) seemed to care does not matter. I received satisfaction from doing it. But he also meant that I should not think just because I liked it and felt good that anyone else really cared. Be careful not to transfer your feelings into the head of another, even a horse. Wow! Profound! Standing in a stable it was just as if Aristotle himself had delivered the lesson for the day.

So humans do things that make them feel better. No surprise. But this is not (always) for selfish reasons; they often project their satisfaction on to others without even realizing they are doing that. Despite the good intentions of many, this can happen even when others are in no way sharing in that satisfaction. Could it be that management programs are put in place that are more about the satisfaction of their authors than they are about satisfying their goal?

What if programs designed for the promotion of diversity and the advancement of women into management positions were really designed to make the incumbents feel better about themselves because they doing something? What's our evidence? Our evidence is that despite program after program and speech after speech, there has been slow progress in the advancement of women in many corporations over the last twenty years.

If the programs have been so ineffective that more than 80 to 90 percent of senior management remain men, then what were these programs designed to do? Why do we continue to maintain these kinds of programs that do not even come close to achieving their stated goals?

The answer might be that corporate management felt better because they were taking action and were seen to be taking action. They felt good about that. But what if the program was, in some cases, never designed to achieve stated goals but only to give a good feeling of having done something?

For some of these programs, the goal was really the appearance of caring about increasing diversity. Senior management would never continue to expend resources in any other aspect of their operations that did not deliver the desired results. They would change their approach over and over again until they got it right. Increasing diversity and the advancement of women in management seems to be an area where some corporations have accepted failure but then on doing the same thing over again each year.

LACK OF "GENDER SUCCESS" IS COSTLY

Today we see that women students occupy more places at our universities than do men, and this trend is growing. What will these women do if they are not hired into good jobs in our businesses? Will they all go into government and the not-for-profit sector? We do not think this is practical or even wise. We expect that the best solution in these industries is a combination of men and women leaders, just as it is in business.

In some university disciplines, the percentage of women taking courses compared with men is almost overwhelming. Do we really think that women will take 60 percent of the degrees in medicine, but be content to let men run health services?

Why would that be a good idea? (We checked, and this is not what's happening. Women play a significant role in health care management.) We should not be surprised to see the same thing happen with respect to law and business. We should expect that the pressure would only accelerate.

But why only react to pressure? Why not instead, seek out the opportunity to act? The failure to act will leave men in 80 to 90 percent of senior roles and will lead to suboptimal corporate performance. The drag on the economy will be substantial.

Countries and competitors that get this right will outperform those that don't. In a world of global competition, it is unwise to forego the advantages that come from adding women to management and boards to work alongside their male counterparts.

THIS IS YOUR TOOLKIT

As you read through the following chapters, you will discover how successful leaders and their companies are moving beyond the limiting perspectives of gender sameness and diversity by numbers.

You'll have the underlying business case for the advancement of women in leadership including the latest financial studies by McKinsey, Credit Suisse, Catalyst, and others that show conclusively that women on boards and on executive teams improve an organization's innovativeness, decision making, productivity, and financial performance.

We're also going to speak to the ascent of women—in science, medicine, education, business, and leadership. We present remarkable statistics on what women have achieved in advanced education and business start-ups. Men are often unaware of these facts; part of the intent of this book is to raise men's awareness of the achievements of women in education and business.

You will be introduced to the neuroscience of gender differences and how those differences play out in the workplace. There's a tidal wave of knowledge coming at us at an increasing rate as technology enables us to peer deeper into the human brain. You'll gain an understanding of the unique ways in which our nature influences men and women's critical thinking skills and their approach to leadership. You'll discover how complementary those differences actually are.

We will share with you the role of the board of directors in effecting change, and we'll examine the correlation between the presence of women on boards and its influence on the presence of women of their company's top management teams.

And we'll bring it all together with solutions to help you rid your company's "plumbing" of bias. We'll show you where and how to address the systemic changes that need to take place within an organization in order to sustain its gender diversity efforts and improve the intake, evaluation, promotion, and ultimate retention of its best talent.

"Barbara, this isn't just a book about increasing gender diversity in the workplace—this book is about fundamental change. It's for male leaders who are unsatisfied with the status quo, are ready to break out of old patterns of behavior, and awaken their organizations to what is possible. It is for leaders who want to achieve what we call 'Gender Success' by deploying women and men together in leadership. This will produce the optimal results."

"It's also for women, Richard, who want to know where and how to invite men in as partners. This is the guidebook that cracks the code on the advancement of women. Give it to every male employee in your firm as their toolkit for understanding the opportunity that exists for them and will help them win."

There's a future coming down like a freight train and companies are positioning themselves for that future. Make sure that you are ready to accept the diverse talent that's knocking at your door.

ENDNOTES

1. Philip Cohen, "How Can We Jump-Start the Struggle for Gender Equality?" *New York Times*, November 23, 2013, https://familyinequality.files.wordpress.com/2013/11/fact-checking-final.pdf.

2. Nancy M. Carter and Christine Silva, "Women in Management: Delusion of Progress," *Harvard Business Review*, March 2010, https://hbr.org/2010/03/women-in-management-delusions-of-progress.

3. Gender Intelligence Group study, "Best Practices in Gender Diversity," 2011.

4. Francesca Lagerberg, "Women in Business: The Path to Leadership," Grant Thornton International Business Report, March 5, 2015, http://www.grantthornton.be/Resources/IBR-2015-Women-in-Business.pdf.

Chapter 2

THE BUSINESS CASE FOR THE ADVANCEMENT OF WOMEN

What if we were to tell you that there is one assured way to improve your financial performance that will not cost you a single penny more than you pay today?

What if your company could be out-competed if your competitors do this before you do?

What if you don't use this strategy and investors shift their investments to competitors that do?

In this chapter, we will share with you the growing body of evidence that proves that companies that advance women into positions of leadership on executive teams and boards perform better than those that don't.

"Richard, there are so many stories that I could share from my own experience on how women in leadership and the creation of cultures of inclusiveness improves the bottom line. Success in today's business environment requires innovative thinking—what we often call *difference thinking*. And the best ideas today are coming from the combination of men and women's unique critical thinking skills.

"One of the many examples of the success of gender-balanced teams and inclusive leadership that stands out for me is at one of the top, global financial services company headquartered in New York City."

"LET'S DO IT!"

It happened while we were facilitating a Gender Intelligence 101 workshop with the company's senior executives. Of the seventeen executives reporting directly to the CEO, four were women. During our co-gender workshops, we typically ask the men and women to form two separate groups to explore and discuss the challenges they experience in working with the other gender. The groups then share their challenges with the entire room and later in the session, after discussing the business case and neuroscience of gender differences, the entire group finds solutions to many of the challenges identified.

One of the challenges that surfaced for women during this special session was that the men on the executive team tended to "kill off potential deals too soon." A new project would surface, the men would typically give it three months to either succeed or fail, and then shift their focus to something else.

The women identified five examples of new projects that were, according to the women, shot down too soon. The four women said, with all confidence, that if the team could revaluate those projects with more long-term thinking and nurturing to success—they could be moneymakers.

The top male leader in the room who had had his own insights that day agreed and said, "Let's do it!"

All five deals were resurfaced and out of those five, four brought about the company's success that year. Readers will discover in Chapter 3, Ascent of Neuroscience, the two strengths in women's hardwiring that often inform women's intuition and developmental instincts—a perfect counterbalance, at times, to men's fact-driven, singular focus.

"Barbara, I believe what you said about cultures of inclusiveness being at the center of all of this. The most successful companies today are creating those cultures and utilizing the skills of every one of their employees. I attribute much of their newfound success and competitiveness to the leadership style of women, something I know we'll be exploring a little later on in this chapter. I have a story as well that speaks to the economic value of that counterbalance.

"Dawn Farrell, CEO of TransAlta Corporation, provides a great example of men and women working together."

At TransAlta, our senior team is comprised of three women and five men. Over the past three years the team has invested $4 billion dollars in new gas and renewable generation, floated a new company, re-sized the company to meet competitive pressures, negotiated an innovative deal for our U.S. coal plant, opened up a significant new front in Western Australia, and invested in our coal technology to improve performance.

Our team includes lawyers, engineers, accountants and economists; we come from different backgrounds and different countries, speaking several languages. We are introverted and extroverted. We dream, strategize, and execute.

Our common ground is that we all work hard to raise our families, contribute to the community, and grow and improve TransAlta. We tease each other about our idiosyncrasies, which can sometimes have a gender bias. This keeps us grounded and laughing. Together, we've trained ourselves to communicate, listen, plan, and lead. There is no other team I'd rather work with.

Companies are starting to view gender balance as a tactical imperative, and they want women in leadership and positions of power because it makes good business sense. A company may reason, for example, that if their products are purchased, in large part, by women, then the organization should have a meaningful representation of women running key business units or heading up departments that better mirror the marketplace.

Our bottom line is that the combination of men and women in leadership roles is a superior arrangement to one without this diversity. The research is compelling—companies that are inclusive of both women and men at all management levels are simply more innovative and productive, and deliver better financial performance.

Acknowledging the diversity advantage and making a concerted effort to recruit, retain, and advance women in conjunction with men helps improve a company's culture and boost its bottom line. And the effect on the bottom line is where we'll begin.

DEFINING SUPERIOR PERFORMANCE

In *Results at the Top*, we are defining "superior performance" as an improvement in any output desired by any stakeholder resulting from actions taken by the firm.

We started out looking only at shareholder value, even though some consider this to be a narrow measure as it only considers earnings, dividends, and share price. Shareholder value could be defined as the sum of all strategic decisions that affect a company's financial performance.

Shareholder value still has a large number of followers. In many companies, the primary drivers that are measured are earnings, dividends, and stock price (or total return to shareholder). They also measured other things such as market share and industry position, but earnings and stock price are clearly the drivers.

When we apply the concept of superior performance to a company in *Results at the Top*, we are using a broader measure. Certainly, everyone would like to see rising earnings and dividends. Ideally, we would like to see a rising stock price; however, rising share prices are often correlated to general economic or industry sector developments rather than a firm's performance. Over and above these traditional measures, we propose to utilize a wide range of performance measures such as inclusive cultures, improved innovativeness and decision making, responsiveness to markets and clients, and minimized risks and costs, all of which we will explore shortly.

ADDING WOMEN TO BOARDS

Let's start with the simple case of adding one woman to a board that is entirely composed of men. Yes, all-male boards still exist but thankfully they are vanishing as the benefits of diversity become more understood. Research tells us that this one addition of a woman director will have a meaningfully positive effect on the performance of the company.

- *Catalyst Research* reported in their 2007 study in conjunction with the Chubb Corporation—covering the period 2001 to 2004—that having at least one woman on the board improved return on equity by 53 percent, return on sales by 42 percent, and return on invested capital by 66 percent.[1]
- *Credit Suisse* reported in both their 2012 and 2014 studies that there was an "outperformance by those companies that had at least one woman on the board when compared to companies with all-male boards." From January 2012 through June 2014, there was an average 5 percent advantage on a sector neutral basis by those companies with at least one woman on the board.[2]

So if one woman added to a company's board improves performance, then what happens when there is more than one? Companies with two or more women directors and also women in top management outperform all-male boards on a variety of financial metrics.

- *McKinsey & Company* examined European companies with market capitalizations of over €150 million for the proportion of women on their executive teams, including their role, their function, and whether there were two or more women on the board of directors. The eighty-nine companies with the highest level of gender diversity were selected and their financial data analyzed. The report observed that, on average, the eighty-nine companies with the highest representation of women outperformed their sector in terms of return on equity (11.4 percent versus an average 10.3 percent); operating result (EBIT of 11.1 percent versus 5.8 percent); and stock price growth (64 percent versus 47 percent) over the period 2005–2007.[3]

The reason women make a powerful difference in the boardroom often ties back to the collaborative leadership style they bring. Their style benefits board dynamics by encouraging directors to attend, listen more carefully, and focus on win-win problem solving. Women are also more likely to ask the tough questions and request direct, detailed answers, which stimulates discussion.

Clearly it matters to corporate leadership and governance that women are on the boards. But is it the mere presence of women that's changing the dialogue and enhancing the decision-making process?

A number of studies reveal that the answer is: not exactly. While one woman can and often does make substantial contributions, and two women are more powerful than one, increasing the number of women to three or more enhances the likelihood that women's voices and ideas are heard. With three or more women, boardroom dynamics are palpably and substantially altered.[4]

Suddenly, having women in board meetings becomes normative. You don't have one or two women representing "a woman's opinion" that could be more easily discounted. Three or more women on a board creates a critical mass where women are no longer seen as outsiders with *their* point of view, but are able to influence the content and process of board discussions more substantially.[5]

Where does the benefit of adding women to the board of companies stop? If the fraction of women continues to increase, when does the marginal performance increase approach zero? The research is not clear on this point. However, by inference, we should conclude that as women begin to dominate boards at above 50 percent of their total composition, then some of the same negative qualities of straight-line thinking that beset boards dominated by men may be evident.

The top of an organization does not just comprise its board of directors: it also includes the company's senior management. What happens to the performance of the firm when you add women to the company's executive team?

- **Dr. Roy Adler,** on behalf of the European Union Commission, conducted an earlier study in 1997 through the European Project on Equal Pay. This study looked at Fortune 500 firms over a nineteen-year period. The purpose was to test whether companies that have a good track record of promoting women to the executive suite were more profitable than those that did not.

  The twenty-five Fortune 500 firms with the best record of promoting women to management positions outperformed the industry median by 34 percent in revenue, 18 percent in asset value, and 26.5 percent in stockholder equity.[6]

- **Catalyst Research**, sponsored by the BMO Financial Group, conducted a study of 353 Fortune 500 companies from 1996 to 2000. "The group of companies with the highest representation of women on their top management teams experienced better financial performance than the group of companies with the lowest representation. The findings were true for the two financial measures of Return on Equity (ROE), which was 35.1 percent higher, and Total Return to Shareholders (TRS), which was 34.0 percent higher.[7]

- **Dezso and Ross**, researchers from the University of Maryland and Columbia Business School, analyzed fifteen years of panel data on the top management teams of the S&P 1,500 firms. Results showed that a given firm generates, on average, one percent (or over $40 million) more economic value with at least one woman on its Top Management Team (TMT) versus companies without any women on the TMT. In addition, women in top management contribute to the innovation intensity of a firm's strategy.[8]

THE REASON FOR THE IMPROVEMENT IN FINANCIAL PERFORMANCE

The results of these and so many other studies are overwhelming and conclusive. Companies that have women representation on their boards and in their senior management realize stronger financial performance.

The bigger question is why? Why is it that the greater the representation of women in senior management and on board, the better the financial performance of companies? There's a reason the bottom line improves, and we've identified four very distinct and significant explanations. Let's look into each.

1. Inclusive cultures
2. Improved innovativeness and decision making
3. Responsiveness to markets and clients
4. Minimized risks and costs

1. Inclusive Cultures

Inclusive cultures source from inclusive leadership, and the pattern of thinking for the past forty years has held that men and women should lead in the same fashion, exemplifying the same time-tested leadership traits.

The workplace has overwhelmingly changed since the 1950s. Yet many of the leadership and management programs, policies, and practices that are still in use today in many large corporations had their beginnings back then with men planning on how to best lead and manage huge workforces composed almost entirely of men.

But what business and scientific research is showing is that there is no truth in the belief that women want or need to lead as men do in order to find success. The only truth is that there are many unfulfilled women not leading from a position of strength. This is something that women in senior leadership are highly attuned to and men are beginning to recognize.

THE FUTURE OF LEADERSHIP

The changing business world actually requires a different kind of leadership today. Conducting business on a global basis is becoming far more competitive, and leadership requires that companies whose enterprises span the globe become less hierarchical and more decentralized in its decision making.

Even teams within organizations are becoming more self-directed. As you'll read later on in this chapter, gender-balanced teams wherein all voices are heard and information and ideas are shared are far more innovative and successful in problem solving than homogeneous teams of all men (or all women, although there are much fewer of those).

In our experience and as reflected in the data, women, and many men, particularly of the millennial generation, prefer working environments that are more collaborative than controlling and that offer teamwork as well as self-directed work. Companies are discovering that if they really want to attract and retain the best talent in the future, the paradigm of leadership to strive toward is one that draws from the common strengths men and women.

Nevertheless, look into the executive conference rooms and on the teams of the majority of companies today and you'll find that the current leadership paradigm that's authoritative, isolating and not collaborative, and singularly focused is still very much in effect, even with the presence of women on those teams.

There's a reason for this that's very instinctive. Under conditions of ambiguity and uncertainty, humans often revert to what they know best, to the old ways of doing things, to what is comfortable. For men, this means employing a more "heroic" style of leadership that is very hierarchical, commanding, and controlling, and focused on solutions and results.

> "Reverting back to the 'old ways,' Richard, reminds me of a client in manufacturing. I really thought the CEO got it when it came to Gender Intelligence and was beginning to walk the talk.
>
> "The CEO's executive staff, one third of which were women, reflected his intentions. Yet his behavior at his company's annual sales conference showed the pitfall that men in leadership often stumble into."

"VALUES DON'T MATTER IF WE'RE NOT MAKING THE NUMBERS"

The CEO took center stage on the first day of the annual sales conference and within the first five minutes of his speech he declared, "I'm so glad that all our employees aspire to our values of collaboration and inclusiveness, but these values won't matter if we're not making the numbers!"

The men in the audience nodded understandingly: "He's right. We have to buckle down and get it done. We've got ninety days to make a difference. We have to move faster on some of our decisions if we want to make our numbers."

The women had a completely different take: "What? Did he just say what I thought I heard him say? These values are not just lip service. It's *what* women value. It's why I'm here! Everyone participating motivates me and improves our productivity. I'm not about quick decisions and success at any cost."

A gender-intelligent CEO would have opened differently by saying, "We need to work harder at being inclusive and bringing our best ideas together. Our values improve our productivity and performance, and inspire us to achieve our results."

> "It may be human nature, Barbara, to revert back to what's comfortable and controlling, but there are many male leaders who are fighting that nature

and succeeding in bigger ways. When we speak of improved innovativeness and decision making, I reflect back to a conversation I had with a male CEO—a person you would most assuredly call a gender-intelligent leader.

"Lance Uggla, CEO of Markit, a global financial information and services company based in London, England, with over 3,600 employees, knew intuitively and recognized the value of gender-balanced teams when it came to problem solving and decision making. And he shared with me how he saw to it that Markit would reflect his beliefs."

> I started my career in banking and, at times, worked in some very male dominated environments that really didn't draw out the organization's strengths. When we started Markit in 2003, we took a conscious decision to create a diverse workplace and as part of that we ensured that we employed women in senior positions. This has not changed to this day. From the perspectives of intellect and capability, women and men are no different. But they do think differently, approach problems differently and have varied but complementary EQ.
>
> As they work together, women and men see the varying qualities and styles in each other and will blend and modify their behavior in an extremely positive way.
>
> When we established our business principles at Markit, I asked one of our senior female employees to lead the discussion. She led a very creative and collaborative project as we explored what we stood for as a company. The process included robust discussions that, if left to a single gender group, would probably have resulted in polarized opinions. However the team drew out the different aspects of our culture in a powerful way.
>
> The approach and perspectives of both women and men were characterized in that work which has subsequently underpinned everything we do.

2. Improved Innovativeness and Decision Making

We do have causal models and arguments that clearly establish the value of diversity of ideas in solving the kinds of complex problems executive teams face all the time. There are a number of studies that really started to spring up around the late 1990s that confirm the power of difference thinking in the field of science. Here are two as example:

- Researchers Hong and Page from the National Academy of Sciences demonstrated in 2004 that groups of diverse problem solvers outperform groups of high-ability problem solvers including homogenous groups of high-IQ individuals. "When dealing with very complicated problems, diversity trumps homogeneous expertise."[9]

- In 2008, Dr. Keith Dunbar from McGill University in Toronto, Canada, presented a new account of the cognitive and social mechanisms underlying complex thinking of creative scientists, and that collections of scientists with very different backgrounds outperform homogeneous groups of scientists.[10]

More recently, behavioral studies at Massachusetts Institute of Technology and Carnegie Mellon University documented the presence of "Collective Intelligence" among groups of people who cooperate well, showing that such intelligence extends beyond the subject matter expert abilities of the groups' individual members (just as in the previous studies) and that the tendency to cooperate effectively together is correlated to the number of women in a group.[11]

The study consisted of 192 teams tasked with solving problems, brainstorming, and decision making. The findings were that the IQ of individuals in a group is not as important to innovative thinking and better decisions as how gender diverse the group is. Also revealed in the data was that the greater the gender diversity of a group, the greater its "Collective Intelligence."[12]

This is not because men and women are so basically different or that women would be more clever, more empathetic, or better than men. It is because women and men bring different viewpoints and experiences to the table and therefore add a richer collection of perspectives and values to the decision-making process.

The research revealed that gender-balanced teams were more prone to listen to each other and be more open-minded. The team members were better able to accept constructive criticism rather than dominating conversations and rushing decisions. The distinctiveness of male and female thinking leads to one conclusion—teams made up of diverse thinking styles produce more creative solutions than that of homogeneous teams, and that diversity of thought is most prevalent in teams that contain a balance of men and women.

In the face of so much data, businesses are ignoring a very important and proven performance lever when they choose to promote homogeneous groups of men to their top management teams and boards of directors. If diversity almost always trumps homogeneity in innovative problem solving and productivity, then not promoting women to executive problem-solving roles becomes a significant opportunity cost!

"You and I both know, Barbara, that dissenters will say that these studies are nothing more than causal models and arguments. That's what amazes me—that we apply a higher standard to gender diversity arguments than we apply to most business norms.

"Why should gender diversity require a higher level of proof than any of the 'self-evident' executive practices we pursue as a matter of course? There are things we know to be true from experience, whatever proofs are put in front of us. Many leaders I know have witnessed the value of diversity of thought. I have as well, and there's one story in particular that stands apart as my proof."

Choosing from Two Ways Forward

One of the most significant management tasks I have undertaken was the replacement of the trading engine at the Toronto Stock Exchange. This was no trivial, everyday decision. Each day, all of Canada's stock trades were routed through these computers. Hundreds of thousands of orders had to be handled flawlessly. The TSE had experienced significant difficulty during the run up and then down of Nortel's shares. The Exchange's trading infrastructure was not able to handle these kinds of volumes and, as a result, was forced to suspend trading in a number of sessions. With great effort, a new trading environment was put in place. The system performed well and permitted the Toronto Stock exchange to demutualize and ultimately to become a public company in 2004.

Of course, when running the company you are never at the end of change. This time the change was external. Innovations in technology and changing regulation were, for the first time in history, creating domestic competitors to the exchange. This competition claimed to offer superior speed and flexibility. Orders coming to the exchange were growing exponentially. We became concerned that our new trading engine, which had been performing so well, would not be up to the job within just a few years.

This is where I was about to learn another lesson. The number two person in the technology division of the exchange, let's call her "Anne," was concerned about the trading infrastructure's capacity to keep up with the potential for new order flow arising from what would come to be called high frequency trading. Her boss was more concerned about reliability and continuous service.

Since the introduction of the new trading engine we had not had a single minute of downtime. Maintaining this record was essential to success. I always remember a comment made that you could fire a pistol into the computer that ran the exchange and it would keep running. This system contained built-in redundancy and failure was unlikely. However, it was not this kind of failure that concerned us. It was the failure that comes about when volumes of orders and trades all try to squeeze down the wire at the same time, overloading systems and triggering a slowdown or complete shutdown of the network feeding the trading computers.

A new system operating on new hardware and software could handle vast quantities of orders and trades. We knew this because US electronic crossing networks deployed this kind of technology. Anne advocated a completely new architecture that adopted this new hardware and operating system. Any transformation of technology on this scale created the possibility of failure. In the exchange business, even minutes of downtime are unacceptable. We called it dial tone reliable. Our clients expected the system to always be ready and able to operate. I had confidence in both of my technology executives. Both were correct in their points of view.

However, as CEO you do not have the luxury of not making a decision. The heat from our new electronic competition was going to be with us for at least the next few years. New customers were expecting message traffic speeds that we could only achieve if we went with new technology. But to change the entire system raised the specter of a failed launch, which, even with minor problems, could cause significant disruption in the market.

We ultimately decided to go with the new infrastructure, as our competitive position was that we supported the market with the best and let traders trade the way they wanted to trade. It cost us our head of technology but now we had a new head of technology. It was the first time a woman had held this position in the history of the exchange. She was committed to the new plan and (as I am certain I reminded her) we were up to our eyeballs in this together.

My support for her never wavered and the new system was ultimately adopted. There were some issues and challenges. These resulted in market outages. But when the system was finally fully in place and tuned for the market it became the fastest and, of course, the dominant system in Canada. The competition could not exploit a technology advantage as we had the best system. This left them with minimal market share and big technology bills to keep up with the leader—us.

"That's a powerful story, Richard. Many male leaders have shared similar experiences with me. Yours is not a story about the superiority of women over men as problem solvers or vice versa. It is a story about men and women working together to achieve a superior outcome.

"You had a strong male leader and a strong female leader making good cases for their positions. By having both positions as genuine alternatives, you increased the strength of your strategy."

3. Responsiveness to Customers and Clients

The third reason for improved financial performance of companies with a better balance of men and women in leadership is market response.

Women represent the largest market opportunity in the world, according to *Forbes* magazine. Globally, they control $20 trillion in annual consumer spending. In the next five years, it is expected that this number will rise to nearly $30 trillion.[13]

Yet many of the marketing strategies, selling techniques, and buying assumptions source from the thoughts and behaviors of men and how they're inclined to sell and buy cars, homes, computers, food, insurance, and health care. Even in companies whose products and services are marketed *exclusively* to women, very few hold any positions of power or, at the very least, influence final decision making over product design and marketing.

Women have an important role as consumers and economic decision-makers. Companies that employ a gender-balanced workforce are better able to identify with and understand the demographics of the marketplace they serve and are better equipped to thrive in that marketplace compared to companies whose solutions and decision making in product design, marketing, and sales are from the perspective of one gender.

"Richard, let me share with you our experiences with financial services companies that speak direct to these statistics. When you combine the facts that women influence 93 percent of financial services decisions yet 84 percent of them feel misunderstood by investment marketers, you have to ask yourself, what are these companies' leaders thinking and doing about it?"

Ignored in Agent-Client Meetings

In survey after survey, women have expressed their dissatisfaction with financial service professionals. They're seldom recognized in agent-client meetings and many don't feel that their particular investment and security needs are being addressed. Even when couples interact with an agent, men are still 58 percent more likely than women to be the primary contact.[14]

As a result, women's dissatisfaction with their agents actually works against the best efforts of companies and agencies looking to build their client base. Women are far more likely than men to refer their favored advisor to family and friends. Over a lifetime, women will, on average, make twenty-six referrals to their financial advisor compared to eleven by the typical male client.[15]

The gap is far wider between women and men when it comes to sharing a negative experience. In our studies over the years, we've discovered that women will tell up to thirty-two other people of a negative experience, whether those people are acquaintances or strangers. Men, on the other hand will only tell up to three people, and only if they're acquaintances.[16]

For as long as advisory firms have been in existence, they have largely catered to men, perhaps because men were traditionally the family breadwinners and in charge of the finances. Those roles are shifting now in many marriages and among single mothers. Women today are taking charge of their finances and creating personal wealth in even greater numbers.

There are more than nine million women-owned businesses in the United States today, accounting for over 50 percent of all privately held enterprises, and over the last twenty years, they've increased in number by 68 percent.[17] Yet the reality that advisors pay more attention to male clients has not changed.

The startling result of all of this misunderstanding is that 70 percent of women fire their male advisor within a year of their husband's death and the majority of them will seek out women advisors instead.[18]

While couples may have similar goals, women's approach to financial planning can be quite different. Many say they feel more comfortable working with other women who understand their needs and are willing to communicate and share their experiences.

For years though, attracting and retaining female agents into the industry has remained a challenge. Today, roughly 30 percent of advisors are women, quite a mismatch to the dynamics that are shaping and defining the future marketplace.[19]

It may be true that women will most often seek women advisors, but they've been left with little choice. The truth is, women will keep their male agents as their trusted advisors and even include men in their search for new advisors, and not female advisors.

They Don't Reflect Our Values

A client of mine, a very gender-diverse company that really walks the talk when it comes to balanced leadership, needed to vet and select a strategic consulting firm for a multimillion-dollar project that would affect the future direction of the company.

They convened a panel of five judges from their executive committee—three women and two men—and proceeded to interview three of the top five global consulting firms. They went through the linear pros and cons and in the end, the men picked two and wanted to move forward and force rank those two to settle on the best of the three. Their rationale was that all three were equally competent and results driven.

The three women judges didn't like any of the firms and voted against all three. The women found their presenters "arrogant and condescending," and ultimately chose a smaller consultancy firm with which to move forward. The women judges also said that their research of the three firms showed that none of the three top consulting firms had gender balance in their leadership.

Additionally, the consulting companies' statistics and stories in the press showed them to be uninviting places for women as consultants and partners. One of the women judges remarked, "We're gender balanced, but that doesn't seem to cross their minds. The presenting teams for all three consulting firms were comprised entirely of men."

Minimized Risks and Costs

Companies will never grow by acting only out of defense; nevertheless, there is the risk of litigation that companies face when failing to meet legal requirements. Sexual discrimination, in all its forms, is a factor that is part of a company's risk assessment. Apart from direct costs, including legal fees and potential fines, there are significant indirect costs such as bad publicity, loss of market share, and damage to the trademark.

The business case for the advancement of women actually extends beyond a company's performance. Every aspect of how a company manages its business is under scrutiny today. In this society, where everyone has a cell phone and everyone can take pictures and recordings, the life of a leader in any organization becomes an open book.

Every time companies and their leaders are seen as doing the right thing—and that includes creating opportunities for people from all backgrounds to thrive within the organization—they add to their credibility with key stakeholders and constituents.

On the other hand, companies that become known as bad employers for women risk a crisis of confidence for their brand and attracting new talent. This can have a negative effect on their survival in an increasingly competitive global economy.

> "Richard, there's something even more subtle here than sexual discrimination. There are times when men don't even know when they've had their vote cancelled by women. And that can negatively impact their own personal career success."

A woman I know is on a board of directors of an oil and gas company headquartered out of the United Kingdom. There are two male directors on the board that she cannot stand and she's letting everyone know it, including the CEO. She's outspoken in sharing that the two male directors don't understand her and are simply and openly dismissive of her.

I know those two men. They are your basic middle-aged men with no experience working with women. They have huge blind spots when it comes to women in business and unfortunately don't know what they don't know or how it's affecting their future with the company.

Unconscious Bias Training—Something's Missing

Diversity training programs, including unconscious bias training, which began around the late 90s, hasn't had the effect for which many have hoped. After two generations of gender diversity training and initiatives, many companies still experience gender discrimination charges.

As the following graph (Figure 2.1) shows, there's been no decline in the number of cases brought as a result of almost a generation of unconscious bias training. In fact, the number of sex-related charges filed with the EEOC has been trending higher over the past eighteen years. [20]

U.S. companies today spend close to $1 billion a year in gender diversity training—a major reason being to prevent lawsuits. Yet, as noted in a recent

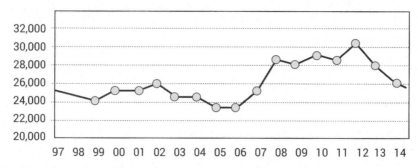

Figure 2.1   Total of Sex-Related Charges, 1997–2015

Harvard Business Review study, most diversity programs are not increasing diversity or minimizing unconscious bias:

> It turns out that while people are easily taught to respond correctly to a questionnaire about bias, they soon forget the right answers. The positive effects of diversity training rarely last beyond a day or two, and a number of studies suggest that it can activate bias or spark a backlash.[21]

"What's interesting is that history has shown that in many sexual discrimination lawsuits, individual suits often turn into class-action with additional women in the organization coming forward with their own stories.

"These are just some of the most recent cases in some of the largest industries that primarily began as a single charge and settled as a class-action lawsuit."

Sexual Discrimination Lawsuits in Consulting and Finance

- KPMG: $400 million (2015)[22]
- Bank of America: $39 million (2013)[23]
- Kleiner Perkins: $16 million (2012)[24]
- Wells Fargo: $32 million (2011)[25]
- Citigroup: $33 million (2008)[26]
- Morgan Stanley: $54 million (2004)[27]

Sexual Discrimination Lawsuits in Pharmaceuticals

- Novartis: $152 million (2010); $110 million (2015)[28]
- Daiichi Sankyo: $8.2 million (2015)[29]
- Merck: $250 million (2014)[30]
- Forest Laboratories: $100 million (2012)[31]
- AstraZeneca: $31 million (2010)[32]

Sexual Discrimination Lawsuits in Technology

Microsoft, Facebook, and Twitter each had individual sexual discrimination charges brought against them in 2015 as attorneys explored if other women would join in the lawsuit.

- **Microsoft** faced a gender discrimination lawsuit filed in September 2015 by a former female employee for alleged gender bias that resulted in lower salaries and lack of promotions for women at the company.[33]
- A former employee of **Facebook** filed a lawsuit in March 2015 accusing the company of gender and racial discrimination as well as sexual harassment.[34]
- At **Twitter**, a former software engineer at the tech firm, also in March 2015, filed a proposed class action lawsuit against the company for not promoting female engineers, like herself, to leadership positions.[35]

This Is So Preventable

Nobody likes litigation. It's painful to the person bringing the claim and it's costly to the person or company trying to defend against the claim. All of this is so preventable. Companies could easily save themselves a ton of money and a ton of agony. What companies need to do is create an environment where this is not happening and the best way to transform corporate cultures is by building knowledge and embedding Gender Intelligence in the leadership mindset and company culture.

"In our experience, Richard, there are three stages in the successful execution of personal development programs: Knowledge, Strategy, and Implementation.

"Yet, much of the diversity training and development of leaders today tends to skip over or offer very little in the way of knowledge building. Typically, information is provided on the intentions of the program and the anticipated outcomes, and then it's implemented across the company.

"As an example, many male leaders share that they don't know how to mentor and sponsor women as opposed to men. Many admit that they don't feel comfortable doing so, regardless of all the gender sameness training they've had in their careers. Yet, they know the value of women in leadership and want to be involved."

Whatever the initiative is, whether talent management, performance feedback, or unconscious bias training, men and women as leaders don't stay in the "knowledge" long enough to remove their blind spots. We will share that knowledge in the chapters to follow and, in Chapter 10, How to Rid the Plumbing of Bias, share how to rid your company of systemic policies and procedures that, in many ways, inadvertently and often unintentionally result in gender discrimination practices.

"Barbara, if women and men are the same, as so many people proclaim, then why is it that leadership, innovation, productivity, and the financial performance of companies improve when there is a greater presence of women on teams, as senior executives, and as board members?"

"Richard, that's an excellent point to bring up at this time, especially given the subject of our next chapter. The reason is because men and women are not the same. These facts are as clear and irrefutable as the business case that we just shared. Men and women don't think the same way. They don't communicate the same way. They don't hear the same things when they are spoken to and they don't mean the same things when they speak. We're designed to be different and to complement each other's differences."

ENDNOTES

1. Catalyst, "The Bottom Line, Connecting Corporate Performance and Gender Diversity," (Catalyst 2004), http://www.catalyst.org/system/files/The_Bottom_Line_Connecting_Corporate_Performance_and_Gender_Diversity.pdf.

2. Julia Dawson, Richard Kersley, and Stefano Natella, "The CS Gender 3000: Women in Senior Management," Credit Suisse AG Research Institute, 2014, http://30percentclub.org/wp-content/uploads/2014/10/2014-09-23_Research_Institute_Women_in_Business.pdf.

3. McKinsey and Company, "Women Matter: Gender Diversity, A Corporate Performance Driver," McKinsey, 2007, http://www.raeng.org.uk/publications/other/women-matter-oct-2007.

4. Vicki W. Kramer, Alison M. Konrad, Sumru Erkut, "Critical Mass on Corporate Boards: Why Three or More Women Enhance Governance," Wellesley Centers for Women, 2006, https://www.wcwonline.org/pdf/CriticalMassExecSummary.pdf.

5. Ibid.

6. Roy D. Adler, "Women in the Executive Suite Correlate to High Profits," European Project on Equal Pay, 1997, Pepperdine University, http://www.csripraktiken.se/files/adler_web.pdf

7. Catalyst, "The Bottom Line."

8. Cristian L. Dezso and David Gaddis Ross, "Does Female Representation in Top Management Improve Firm Performance? A Panel Data Investigation," *Strategic Management Journal* 33, no. 9, 2012, 12, https://www0.gsb.columbia.edu/mygsb/faculty/research/pubfiles/3063/female_representation.pdf.

9. Lu Hong and Scott E. Page, "Groups of Diverse Problem Solvers Can Outperform Groups of High-Ability Problem Solvers, *Proceedings of the National Academy of Sciences,* vol 101, no. 46, November 2004, http://www.pnas.org/content/101/46/16385.full.

10. Kevin Dunbar, "How Scientists Think: On-line Creativity and Conceptual Change in Science," McGill University, 2008, http://www.cc.gatech.edu/classes/AY2013/cs7601_spring/papers/Dunbar.pdf

11. Anita Williams Woolley, Christopher F. Chabris, Alex Pentland, Nada Hashmi, Thomas W. Malone, "Evidence for a Collective Intelligence Factor in the Performance of Human Groups: Number of Women in Group Linked to Effectiveness in Solving Difficult Problems," *Science Daily,* October 29, 2010, Volume 330, p 686, http://www.chabris.com/Woolley2010a.pdf.

12. Ibid.

13. Jennifer Gilhool, "The Power of 'Just One Woman,'" *Forbes Magazine*, August 26, 2013, http://www.forbes.com/sites/85broads/2013/08/26/the-power-of-just-one-woman/#15457e4e7893.

14. "Fidelity Study Finds Men 58 Percent More Likely to Drive Financial Advisor Relationships," December 2013, https://www.fidelity.com/about-fidelity/corporate/fidelity-study-finds-men-58-percent-more-likely.

15. Andrew Osterland, "Female Clients More Likely Than Men to Make Referrals," *Investment News*, April 24, 2012, http://www.investmentnews.com/article/20120424/FREE/120429972/female-clients-more-likely-than-men-to-make-referrals.

16. Gender Intelligent Group Surveys: 2005–2015.

17. American Express, "State of Women-Owned Businesses Report," March 2014, http://www.womenable.com/content/userfiles/2014_State_of_Women-owned_Businesses_public.pdf.

18. Melissa J. Anderson, "Why the Financial Advisor Industry Needs Women," *The Glass Hammer*, http://theglasshammer.com/2013/03/19/why-the-financial-advisor-industry-needs-women/.

19. Bureau of Labor and Statistics, Household Data, Annual Averages: Table 11, http://www.bls.gov/cps/cpsaat11.pdf.

20. Equal Employment Opportunity Commission Sex-Based Charges FY 1997–2014, https://www.eeoc.gov/eeoc/statistics/enforcement/sex.cfm.

21. Frank Dobbin and Alexandra Kalev, "Why Diversity Programs Fail," *Harvard Business Review*, July-August, 2016, https://hbr.org/2016/07/why-diversity-programs-fail.

22. Kelly Knaub, "Law 360, February 19, 2015," http://www.law360.com/articles/623251/equitable-tolling-sought-in-400m-kpmg-sex-bias-suit.

23. Jonathan Stempel and Nate Raymond, "Bank of America's Gender Bias Settlement Approved by Court," *Chicago Tribune*, December 27, 2013, http://articles.chicagotribune.com/2013-12-27/news/sns-rt-bankofamerica-biassettlement-20131227_1_bank-brokers-bias.

24. David Streitfeld, "Ellen Pao Loses Silicon Valley Bias Case Against Kleiner Perkins," *The New York Times*, March 2015, http://www.nytimes.com/2015/03/28/technology/ellen-pao-kleiner-perkins-case-decision.html?_r=0.

25. Jennifer Hoyt Cummings, "Wells Fargo Reaches Settlement in Gender-Bias Suit," *Wall Street Journal*, June 9, 2011, http://www.wsj.com/articles/SB10001424052702304259304576375520007891038.

26. Associated Press, "Citi Pays $33M to Settle Discrimination Suit," *Crane's Business*, April 4, 2008, http://www.crainsnewyork.com/article/20080404/FREE/416027371/citi-pays-33m-to-settle-discrimination-suit.

27. Patrick McGeehan, "Morgan Stanley Settles Sex Bias Lawsuit," *The New York Times*, July 13, 2004, http://www.nytimes.com/2004/07/13/business/morgan-stanley-settles-bias-suit-with-54-million.html.

28. Ed Silverman, "Novartis Division Is Charged with Sex Discrimination," *Wall Street Journal*, March 18, 2015, http://blogs.wsj.com/pharmalot/2015/03/18/novartis-division-is-charged-with-sex-discrimination-by-former-employees/.

29. Beth Winegarner, "Daiichi Sankyo Shells Out $8.2M in Sex Bias Settlement," *360Law*, August 31, 2015, http://www.law360.com/articles/697235/daiichi-sankyo-shells-out-8-2m-in-sex-bias-settlement.

30. Joshue Alston, "Merck Gender Bias Suit Swells to $250M after Plaintiffs Added," *360Law*, January 17, 2014, http://www.law360.com/articles/502194/merck-gender-bias-suit-swells-to-250m-after-plaintiffs-added.

31. "$100 Million Gender Discrimination Class Action Filed Against Forest Laboratories," July 6, 2012, https://www.bigclassaction.com/lawsuit/forest-pharmaceuticals-gender-discrimination-class.php.

32. Erik Greb, "AstraZeneca Settles Sex-Discrimination Lawsuit," *BioPharm International*, June 14, 2011, http://www.biopharminternational.com/astrazeneca-settles-sex-discrimination-lawsuit-0.

33. Leena Rao, "Microsoft Hit with Gender Discrimination Suit," *Fortune*, September 16, 2015, http://fortune.com/2015/09/16/microsoft-gender-discrimination-suit/.

34. Tom Huddleston, Jr., "Facebook Is Sued for Sex Discrimination, Harassment," *Fortune Magazine*, March 18, 2015, http://fortune.com/2015/03/18/facebook-sex-discrimination/.

35. Sarah Ashley O'Brien, "Twitter Is Latest Tech Firm Sued for Sex Discrimination," *CNN Money*, March 24, 2015, http://money.cnn.com/2015/03/24/technology/twitter-sex-discrimination-lawsuit/.

Chapter 3

ASCENT OF NEUROSCIENCE

"The past decade witnessed tremendous growth in the evidence for potent sex influences on the brain at all levels of its function, down to the molecular level. The domain of emotional memory is no exception.

"The general conclusion is that the burden of proof on the sex influence issue, both for those studying emotional memory and for neuroscience in general, has shifted: from those pursuing the issue generally having to justify why, to those not doing so having to justify why not."

— Dr. Larry Cahill[1]

There are three dynamic events under way in our world today, and from the standpoint of where we are ultimately headed in leadership in industry and in government, they're all related.

We spoke of the ascent of women in dominating education, acquiring advanced degrees in all fields of study, and moving into positions of leadership. We celebrated the ascent of men in their advocacy for more women in leadership. More and more male leaders are acknowledging the business case for gender diversity and the advancement of women in leadership roles in their companies and industries.

The third happening is the tidal wave of new knowledge coming at us at an increasing rate as technology enables us to peer more deeply into the functioning of the brain and mind. Dr. Larry Cahill's point about the burden of proof shifting signifies the abundance of evidence that neurological sex differences influence the differing thoughts and actions of men and women. It challenges researchers and clinicians who are still resisting the evidence to prove otherwise.

EQUAL DOES NOT MEAN THE SAME!

"Richard, what is at the root of the resistance to accepting that men and women are neurologically different is a deeply ingrained assumption that if men and women are equal, then men and women must be the same and therefore should be regarded and treated the same.

"This is, with all the best of intentions, a false and harmful assumption. The truth is that of course men and women are equal, all human beings are equal, but that doesn't mean that they're the same. Equal does not mean they have to be the same or act the same.

"This false assumption has led us down the wrong path for decades to the point where today, women and men, even boys and girls, are *not* being treated equally or authentically, which is actually stifling their natural talents and impulses. This is a huge blind spot for many people: women are being treated as if they are the same as men and are even evaluated and promoted (unknowingly of course) on the basis of how well they perform as men!"

THE ASCENT OF NEUROSCIENCE

Since the 1990s, doctors, neuroscientists, psychologists, and anthropologists have produced a remarkable body of work identifying brain differences between the sexes—differences that influence men's and women's perceptions of the world, their thoughts, and their behaviors. They've also discovered what fuels these differences is our biochemistry and the interplay of hormones with brain structures that are already wired to react to those hormones.

The real breakthrough is in recognizing how these differences inform the ways in which men and women communicate and listen, deal with stress, handle day-to-day conflict, address issues and challenges, and make decisions.

Of course family, education, and culture all shape us from birth, but generations of nurturing most often parallel what is already natural within us, and we as parents and educators attempt to modify that nature in order to coexist with changing social norms. As an example, mothers today may coach their young sons who show aggressive tendencies to be less forceful while fathers may encourage their daughters who tend to be quiet to be more outspoken.

THE DOMINO EFFECT

"Richard, a term that I've been using for years to describe the awakening that takes place in people once they're exposed to the neuroscience that underlies gender differences is 'The Domino Effect,' because, just as in dominos, lines of reasoning and assumptions begin to fall.

"We've seen it in our Gender Intelligence Group practice for years. Understanding our differences leads to accepting, valuing, and engaging those differences. Once men are exposed to the business case and the brain science, they go through an epiphany—an awakening. Many make the connection through personal life experiences and situations. Once they become aware, it seems as if a weight is lifted off of the their shoulders. They feel freer—freer to be themselves and have authentic conversations."

This book is written primarily for men, to help them become better at engaging and working with women; however, it's also a guide for women in how to engage and work better with men. Women and men have been going about it the wrong way for quite a while now. We provide a path to better understand and be better understood by the other gender.

BELL CURVE OF GENDER TENDENCIES

When we speak of gender differences and tendencies in critical thinking, we're describing a bell curve of "thought and action" *tendencies* in men and "thought and action" *tendencies* in women.

This means there is a distribution of behavior along a continuum with the greatest number of people exhibiting tendencies that fall toward the middle or norm. In layperson's terms, if we organized all men on a continuum from factual to intuitive, more of them would fall toward the fact-based side of midpoint, whereas the average for women would be closer to the intuitive side.

When you place these two bell curves alongside each other (see Figure 3.1), you'll notice a huge difference between the average tendencies in how men think and act and the average tendencies in how women think and act.

You'll also notice that there is some overlap. About 20 percent of us are hardwired more like the opposite gender.

Given the distribution of human dynamics along this curve, it would be a gross generalization to claim that all men are one way and all women are another. After all, there is a lot of overlap on the graph.

Actually, it would be more wrong to say that we're all the same—if not for upbringing, education, and culture. The reality is that we're more different than the same in many ways, and that fact is driven by hardwired differences in our brain structures and in our hormonal composition. What are some of the ways these differences show themselves?

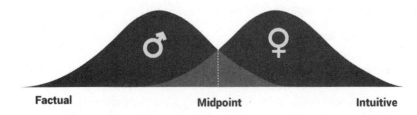

Factual   **Midpoint**   **Intuitive**

Figure 3.1   The Bell Curve of Gender Tendencies

- Women tend to take a more intuitive approach to their environment, which stems from an ability to perceive people and events more deeply and with greater memory capacity. Men tend to take a more fact-based surface approach to their environment, more often scanning for challenges and threats.
- In problem solving, men tend to converge in their thinking, define and declare the problem, and begin eliminating and isolating issues. Women will often define the problem in broader terms and allow a wider array of potential factors.
- Men and women tend to deal with conflict differently. The stress associated with conflict only enhances each gender's natural, and in many ways, unconscious ways of dealing with emotional issues. Our bodies' natural pursuit of homeostasis strives to reduce stress and find balance. Men tend to depersonalize and externalize the issue, giving them time to think through solutions, often in solitude, whereas women tend to personalize and are more inclined to want to talk through the issue to reach understanding.

Some women do make it to the top of companies, to a large extent because the male model authentically fits their bridge brain.

Although we're establishing that there are hardwired differences in the brain structures of males and females, it is not a hard and fast rule that all men are one way and all women another. There are exceptions to the rule. The term "bridge brain" is used to include those people whose brains share a number of characteristics of the other gender's brain, or those men and women who just sense that their brains may be more toward the middle of the bell curve of gender tendencies. However, a predominant number of women climb the corporate ladder only to find that they don't fit the mold and couldn't if they tried. Many simply don't want to compromise their authenticity. More important, if we try to get them to fit the mold, it also means we are not taking advantage of the strengths that women's different critical thinking skills can offer.

THE ABILITY TO PEER MORE DEEPLY

MRI studies have shown that the regions of the male and female brain activate differently, no matter the person's culture or country of origin. Only since the mid- to late 1990s have scientists been able to "image" blood flow in milliseconds and track how and where thoughts activate blood and hormone streams.

Figure 3.2 shows blood flow through regions of the male and female brain while at rest. It's pretty amazing. Once a workshop group or audience sees this and hears the explanation, they begin to realize that there truly are innate differences between men and women, deeper than upbringing and culture.

At rest, women's brains tend to be more active than men's and are often filled with more thoughts. Women will tend to want to interact with colleagues after a stressful meeting or interact with family, friends, or relatives at the end of a

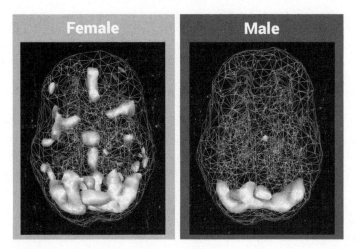

Figure 3.2 The Brain at Rest
Source: MRI scans courtesy Dr. Daniel Amen, Amen Clinic.

busy day. These activities help women produce oxytocin, increase relaxation, and relieve stress, which in itself produces even more oxytocin, a critical stress-reducing hormone that we will discuss in more depth later.

After a long or stressful meeting or at the end of a busy day, men tend to want to shut down and drift off—close off the world for a little while. Men tend to retreat and seek solitude or engage in some low-involvement activity such as watching the news or sports, or working on a small project. It's a natural tendency in a man to "turn off" in order to replenish testosterone, and that relieves his stress, relaxes, and reenergizes him. You can even see that behavior in young boys.

It's not that men are empty-headed or don't care about the events around them when they seem not to pay attention, don't respond, or don't show enough emotion, or when they even fail to remember important occasions, tasks, conversations, or even past arguments. Men's thoughts and actions are often centered on disengaging in order to reduce stress, especially if there are no challenges or threats from the immediate environment.

Nothing is black and white though. There are women who relax through solitude and men who like to socialize. What's fascinating and truly worth knowing is the "why" behind our predominate tendencies.

Knowing that there are reasons why we often think and act the way we do helps both men and women be more "actively conscious" of what's motivating the other gender and themselves in their business and personal relationships. This helps men and women appreciate what the other gender is naturally seeking after a stressful meeting, or in the midst of a conflict, or at the end of a busy day. The greatest importance is in understanding how these gender differences manifest themselves so that we don't misinterpret them when they show up in the workplace or in our personal lives.

SEX DIFFERENCES IN BRAIN STRUCTURE AND FUNCTION

The brain is an interconnected computer that processes information through a combination of brain regions and biochemistry. No one part acts alone. We can now associate functions to specific regions of the brain and, in doing so, reveal some of the most meaningful areas of difference between men and women—differences that have found a natural balance as we've evolved together for the past six million years.[2]

While there are many parts of the brain that reflect variations by gender, in our work we find it valuable to concentrate on seven main areas of significance. We'll explain the science behind each part, but more important, how it shows up in our day-to-day lives.

Prefrontal Cortex

If it appears that girls tend to mature faster than boys or that women are more careful in their decision making than men, it is because this is true. The **prefrontal cortex**—the part of our brains that controls judgment, decision making, and consequential thinking—is much larger in women than in men and develops faster in girls than in boys.[3]

The prefrontal cortex is the judgment center of the brain and moderates and controls social behavior, decision making, and action. The underlying differences between men's larger amygdala, a region we'll cover shortly, and their smaller prefrontal cortex speak to some of the reasons young boys tend to be more exploratory and take more risks than young girls—a tendency in males that can continue well into their adult lives.

During meetings, women will often include more details in their decision making, and they'll verbalize those details during meetings or in conversations. This is often misinterpreted by male peers to mean that women's deliberations take more time when they actually do not.

Corpus Callosum

The corpus callosum is a part of the brain that plays a very significant role in how we process information. The brain is divided into two hemispheres: the right brain, the basis of intuitive, holistic, and creative thought; and the left brain, the source of linear, logical, and serial thinking. The corpus callosum is a thick bundle of nerves connecting both halves.

Where women tend to engage in right-brained and left-brained activities simultaneously and blend facts with intuition, men tend to use their brain halves sequentially. One of the factors that enable this "whole-brain" thinking in women is that the corpus callosum is 25 percent larger on average in female brains than in male brains and is shaped differently. The female corpus callosum also contains more nerve fibers and white matter that enable women to travel back and forth between the left and right sides more fluidly.[4]

Dr. Helen Fisher, biological anthropologist at the Center for Human Evolutionary Studies in the Department of Anthropology, Rutgers University, has been on the national and international lecture circuit since 1983, speaking to the evolution of human sexuality, gender differences, and the future of men and women in business and family life.

In her book, *The First Sex: The Natural Talents of Women and How They Are Changing the World*, Helen describes the effect of the corpus callosum on women's contextual thought processes and contrasts it to men's inclination to think in a more serial, stepwise fashion.

> I think the most dramatic difference between the sexes is how they think. When women think, they collect more pieces of information and put that information into more complex patterns. They see more relationships between patterns and they weigh more variations before they come up with their decisions on how to proceed. Women tend to think contextually, holistically. They think in webs of factors. Not straight lines.
>
> Men are more likely to do what I call step-thinking. They will focus on a particular issue, they'll get rid of extraneous data, and they will move in a more step-like fashion towards the goal.[5]

Anterior Cortex

As with the corpus callosum, and adjacent to it, women generally have a larger anterior cortex than men, a difference to which many scientists attribute women's ability to integrate and arrange memories and emotions into more complex patterns of thought, weigh more variables, and consider a wider array of options and solutions to an issue. As a result, women tend to reflect (ruminate) and express concerns more often than men do. For this reason, the anterior cortex is also known as the "worrywart" center of the brain, and research demonstrates that anxiety is more common in women than in men.[6]

Brain scan studies also indicate that through the anterior cortex, the female brain has a larger areas of sensitivity with which to track their intuitions. It turns out that "women's intuition" is actually real and grounded in biology.[7]

> "Intuition, Richard, has been undervalued in women in business and many other areas of life. But it is a biological fact that women, for the most part, are more emotional and empathetic than men.
>
> "In meetings, women are more likely than their male counterparts to read the facial expressions of the people around them and take the temperature of the room, which offers them greater insight into what's happening around them. These feelings produce an intuition, a sensitivity within which women need to learn to place more trust.
>
> "A senior executive male leader in investment banking shared one of the insights that he had about ten years ago, around the time he really started

listening to the three women colleagues on his executive team comprised of twelve people."

"Barbara, I was also so focused on the results and the data. And often ignored 'people issues' as they arose. We then all underwent a 360-degree leadership assessment and I rated myself a nine out of ten on my leadership and the three women on my committee rated me a three! I was floored.

"The reason the women on my team rated me that low was because I was treating everyone the same and I wasn't listening. They had a much better line of sight into what was happening with the team and with each executive on it. It was quite an awareness I never had before or knew to value. That is a gift women can bring."

Insula

The role of insula (also known as the insular cortex), which is found within each hemisphere of the brain and no larger than a fingernail, is very complex. The insula informs our emotional response to our surroundings, helps us control our heartbeat and blood pressure, modulates basic functions like swallowing and speech, and even governs our very consciousness and sense of self.[8]

The insula is, on average, twice as large in the female brain as in the male brain, helping women translate physical sensations and thoughts in the subconscious mind into conscious thoughts that are captured as memories and emotions. The insula enables women to draw on past memories and learn from them, preventing women from acting hastily and taking unnecessary risks.[9]

Much like the way middleware interacts with mainframes, the insula acts in conjunction with the hippocampus, which we'll talk about next. The interplay of these two systems enables women to draw on past memories, identify patterns, and make immediate connections.

Hippocampus

The hippocampus is the center for long-term emotional memory, and is almost twice as large and more active in women than in men. This, along with the insula, helps to explain why women tend to be far better at recalling intricate details of past experiences and make immediate connections and visualize patterns in past experiences.[10]

Possessing a larger hippocampus also enables women to be more effective at processing and coding emotional experiences into their long-term memory. In the business world, that rich, interwoven database of experiences can be highly useful in looking for causes and solutions. However, that same connection can also manifest in a negative manner by making women more hesitant in their decision-making process.

"This, Richard, is a perfect example of that counterbalance I spoke of at the onset of this section. I was invited to attend a product launch strategy session with a rather large high-tech company in Silicon Valley. The chief technology officer and sales director, both men, were challenging their teams and wanted to see results in the next quarter.

"Two women from the IT organization tried in vain to bring to the group's attention the failure of a similar launch a year ago because tech support and client training weren't prepared. And, as it turns out, the training and support center were behind and needed more time. The women suggested the team delay the launch for another month."

Amygdala

The amygdala is located in the limbic system, the oldest part of our brain, and is best known for governing our "flight or fight" response to fear, danger, or stress. Influenced by hormones, the amygdala processes fear and triggers aggression and action. It alerts us to danger and switches on the rest of the body, preparing us to deal appropriately with the situation.

The amygdala is significantly larger and more active in men's brains than in women's. Moreover, because of hormonal differences, men and women also tend to respond differently to fear signals coming from the amygdala.[11]

"Richard, I know we spend a lot of time talking about the collaborative-thinking value that women bring to the problem solving and decision-making processes, but I have to tell you, there are times when the way men think is of greater value.

"I'm currently working with a team of six leaders at a financial services firm representing wholesale banking and community (retail) banking. The team is made up of five women and one man. During our periodic calls, I can hear the male leader express his frustrations as if there's no tomorrow. Then he goes on mute, I think just to contain himself.

"I've spoken with him in one-on-ones and he honestly shares with me that he can't handle the amount of detailed overprocessing that women engage in, and the attention given to each minute detail of an issue.

"The female brain can be just as dominating as the male brain and at times, not as productive because women can get bogged down in the minu-tiae. Women tend to over-diverge and there is the need for the balancing male brain saying, 'Let's move to action on this and check it off the list.'"

Cerebellum

As we just noted, the amygdala has direct neural connections to other response areas in the brain—primarily, the cerebellum and its regulation of motor control. The cerebellum may also be involved in cognitive functions such as attention and language and in regulating fear and pleasure responses. The cere-bellum doesn't initiate movement, but it contributes to coordination, precision, and accurate timing. It receives input from sensory systems of the spinal cord and from other parts of the brain, and integrates these inputs fine-tune motor activity.[12]

In addition to aiding men's reaction time and fluidity, the greater size of the cerebellum in men influences them to communicate more nonverbally than women, with more emphasis on movement and physicality than on words.[13]

SEX DIFFERENCES IN HORMONAL COMPOSITION

Just as variations in our behavioral tendencies are explained by differences in men and women's brain structure, the roles and volume of certain hormones also help explain gender differences, especially in how men and women deal with stress.

Men and women produce all the same hormones; there are no hormones that are specific to men or specific to women. We just produce different amounts, and it's the difference in those levels that produces distinct effects in each gender.

When you couple the differences in brain structure and function with varying hormonal levels, the differences in the thoughts and actions of males and females becomes even more accentuated. Let's look at the effect of differences in three key hormones: testosterone, oxytocin, and cortisol.

Testosterone

Testosterone, the principle male sex hormone, is one of the key elements in determining the sexual characteristics in men including physical strength, body shape, deeper voice, and sexual drive. Testosterone is not simply the fuel for aggressive behavior. It also plays an important role in men's drive, competitiveness, creativity, intellect, and in their ability to develop and execute new ideas. More than anything, having the right level of testosterone is essential to help men cope appropriately with stress.[14]

Women also produce testosterone, though men typically produce twenty to thirty times more than women do, but the hormone does not function in the same stress-reducing manner that it does in men.

Normal levels of testosterone are linked to feelings of success in men. When men face difficulty or failure, their testosterone levels will begin to drop and they'll experience lowered spirits or even feel depressed until their levels are replenished.

This dynamic also defines some of the reason why men will often ignore a difficult problem. Avoiding the issue or shutting down gives them time to think through the issue, oftentimes in solitude. This allows men to recoup and replenish their testosterone levels and gain the mental strength and drive to tackle the issue.

Oxytocin

Oxytocin, also known as the social attachment hormone, is produced in great quantities in women during childbirth and in both women and men during orgasm. The hormone affects social recognition and bonding as well as the formation of trust between people.

Oxytocin also reduces blood pressure, feelings of fear, and levels of cortisol, a hormone produced by the adrenal glands in both men and women. In women, oxytocin levels can rise during a relaxing conversation and fall in response to feeling ignored or abandoned.

While oxytocin works to lower stress levels in women, in men, too much oxytocin can actually reduce testosterone levels and thereby increase their stress. Alternately, too much testosterone in women can reduce the effectiveness with which oxytocin functions in their bodies.[15]

This may be why men will tend to seek solitude in times of stress as conversation can often add to their stress, whereas women will tend to seek conversation as solitude can often add to their stress levels.

Cortisol

Cortisol is a natural and helpful part of the body's response to stress, though higher and prolonged levels in the bloodstream can also have its negative effects. Cortisol plays an important function in the body, from glucose metabolism to the regulation of blood pressure, blood-sugar maintenance, and the functioning of the immune system.[16]

Too much cortisol can cause an increase in blood pressure and blood sugar levels, and even add more fat around the belly. High levels of cortisol can also lead to impaired cognitive performance or an inability to think clearly.

Oxytocin-producing activities in women work to lower cortisol levels and reduce stress. But when women aren't able to collaborate at work, or there's not enough time to attend to personal life events and needs, their stress and anxiety will increase beyond their ability to relax and collect themselves. That increase in stress brought on by the rush of cortisol stimulates the production of testosterone in women's systems and inhibits their ability to produce oxytocin, thereby perpetuating the stress cycle. [17]

Elevated cortisol levels can have a draining effect on men as well, depleting their testosterone levels and increasing their blood pressure, anxiety, irritability, and fatigue. It can also cause weight gain in men. However, studies have shown that women pay the greater price nowadays. Women's cortisol levels at work tend to be twice as high as men's, and at home, their levels can be four times higher.[18]

"Richard, speaking of stress, here is a story that many of us are aware of and have experienced, and which I think shows how the best of both minds, working together, under extremely stressful times, produced the best possible outcomes in terms of preparedness."

THE BREAKTHROUGH THAT KNOWLEDGE BRINGS

"What could the world look and act like if we took the best of both styles, bringing together men and women's unique and highly complementary minds to the benefit of business and governments around the world?

"Appreciating and valuing our differences creates an indelible shift in our attitudes and behaviors—a remarkable change, even in self-perception. I can't tell you how many times when I share the science with senior women, they say, 'I thought there was something wrong with me. I thought I just couldn't fit.'

"Women find the science so validating of the way they think and act. Men, on the other hand, haven't wanted to engage in conversations about their behavior. They didn't want to talk about it for the longest time because it's mostly about their male paradigms and placing blame, and insisting that men need to change. Who wants to engage in that kind of conversation?

"But introduce the science and men light up and sit forward in their chairs, completely engaged. Men tell me that this knowledge, that knowing that they are wired for a reason, has freed them. Let me explain what I mean. Oftentimes in personal relationships, women will work on trying to get men to be more like their girlfriends. But once they understand the neuroscience underlying the differences, women begin to honor the difference in men and that allows men the freedom to be themselves and have authentic conversations and not politically correct conversations with women.

"That's the breakthrough that understanding the science creates—men and women understanding each other and working more productively together because of it. This awareness and valuing of our hardwired differences has also helped us improve our patience and understanding as couples, and in our efforts as parents, looking to raise sons and daughters to become authentic men and women."

ENDNOTES

1. Larry Cahill, "Sex Influences on Brain and Emotional Memory: The Burden of Proof has Shifted," Neuroscience Brown Bag Series, Vanderbilt University, January 15, 2015, https://events.vanderbilt.edu/index.php?eID=58201.

2. Nadia Drake, "Human Evolution 101," *National Geographic*, September 11, 2015, http://news.nationalgeographic.com/2015/09/human-evolution-101/.

3. Deborah Blum, *Sex on the Brain: The Biological Differences Between Men and Women* (New York: Viking, 1997), 63.

4. Louann Brizendine, *The Female Brain* (New York: Three Rivers Press/ Crown, 2007), 64–65.

5. Helen Fisher, *The First Sex: The Natural Talents of Women and How They Are Changing the World* (New York: Random House, 2007), 9.

6. J. Decety, and P. L. Jackson, "The Functional Architecture of Human Empathy," *Behavioral and Cognitive Neuroscience Review* 3, no. 2 (2004): 71–100.

7. Women's Intuition Is Biological: Lower Exposure to Testosterone in the Womb Gives Females an Extra 'Sense,'" *Daily Mail*, April 24, 2014, http://

www.dailymail.co.uk/sciencetech/article-2612317/Womens-intuition-bio
logical-Lower-prenatal-exposure-testosterone-makes-women-intuitive-men
.html.

8. Sarah Griffiths, "Women Outperform Men When Identifying Emotions,"
   Science Daily, October 21, 2009, https://www.sciencedaily.com/releases/
   2009/10/091021125133.htm.

9. Brizendine, *The Female Brain*, 120.

10. Zeenat F. Zaidi, "Gender Differences in the Human Brain: A Review,"
    The Open Anatomy Journal 2 (2010): 37–55, https://www.researchgate.net/
    publication/228549134_Gender_Differences_in_Human_Brain_A_Review.

11. Stephan Hamann, "Sex Differences in the Responses of the Human Amyg-
    dala," *The Neuroscientist* vol.11, no. 4 (2005): 290, http://languagelog.ldc
    .upenn.edu/myl/ldc/llog/Brizendine/Hamann2005.pdf.

12. Uri Wolf, Mark Rapoport, Tom Schweizer, "Evaluating the Affective
    Component of the Cerebellar Cognitive Affective Syndrome," *Journal of
    Neuropsychiatry and Clinical Neurosciences* 21, no. 3 (2009): 245–253.

13. Detlef Heck, Fahad Sultan, "Cerebellar Structure and Function: Making
    Sense of Parallel Fibers," *Human Movement Science* 21 (2002): 411–421,
    http://keck.ucsf.edu/~houde/sensorimotor_jc/DHeck02a.pdf.

14. Fiona McPherson"The Role of Emotion in Memory," http://www.memory-
    key.com/memory/emotion.

15. Tori DeAngelis, "The Two Faces of Oxytocin," *American Psychological
    Association* 39, no. 2 (2008): 30, http://www.apa.org/monitor/feb08/oxytocin
    .aspx.

16. Elizabeth Scott, "Cortisol and Stress: How to Stay Healthy," September 22,
    2011, http://stress.about.com/od/stresshealth/a/cortisol.htm.

17. Michael Randall, "The Physiology of Stress: Cortisol and the Hypothalamic-
    Pituitary-Adrenal Axis," *Dartmouth Undergraduate Journal of Science*,
    February 3, 2011, http://dujs.dartmouth.edu/fall-2010/the-physiology-of-
    stress-cortisol-and-the-hypothalamic-pituitary-adrenal-axis.

18. Vikram Patel, Alistair Woodward, Valery Feigin, Stella R. Quah, and Kristian
    Heggenhougen, "*Mental and Neurological Public Health: A Global Perspec-
    tive*," (Cambridge: Academic Press April 19, 2010), 5.

Chapter 4

ASCENT OF WOMEN

Over the past thirty years, women's achievements in science, medicine, education, business, and leadership have been nothing short of spectacular. There are amazing statistics that we will review in this chapter on what women globally have achieved in advanced education and leadership positions. Many men and women are unaware of women's achievements, particularly in advanced education, and the intent of this book is to raise that level of awareness.

While writing this book, we learned of Germany's decision to adopt a quota of 30 percent women on supervisory boards in that country's hundred largest companies. In addition, thirty-five hundred large German firms will be required to announce public targets for increasing the number of women in management roles. Should we be pleased to see this decision in Germany, or saddened by it?

On the one hand, this will finally get German companies to do something they should have done anyway. On the other hand, we have the oversight of government once more intervening in business because society believes there has been a market failure. There's little indication that German companies would have done this anyway. A former executive at Deutsche Telekom was quoted as saying, "Those issues were not at the core of the discussion. Everybody thought that's a wave that is going to pass."

Many men do not yet see a reason to change. They see gender diversity as a fad—just as the Deutsche Telkom executive said.

Time, though, will take care of those who do not want to change, just as it does with everything else that can't adapt to its changing environment. In any case, a little time is nothing compared to the length of time women have had to wait for equality to come to their lives and work experience.

THE FIRST LONG STEP

When examining any issue as complex as the relationship between men and women in organizations today, you need to include an understanding of the historical context. We don't mean going back to the Garden of Eden to examine the dynamics of that particular relationship. But we do have to understand the forces that changed the attitudes regarding women's right to vote.

For those of you unfamiliar with this chapter of history, let us remind you that our grandmothers and great-grandmothers may have participated directly in this debate in countries such as the United States, Canada, and the United Kingdom. But for many women today across the globe, this battle is still very real.

The assumption many of us make is that women have had the right to vote for hundreds of years, when in reality, suffrage only came to women in the majority of the world in the middle to latter half of the twentieth century. They won it in Switzerland in 1971, in South Africa in 1994, in the UAE in 2006, and in Saudi Arabia in 2011.[1]

Think about it for a moment: How would you men out there feel if you were denied the right to vote? What if you had faced these circumstances because you were a man? Fine for you to work and contribute to society on our farms and factories, and in raising families, but when it comes to setting public policy, you're not required! Yet women were expected to be fine with this arrangement.

"I can hear the critics now, Barbara, asking me what's wrong with me. They'll say that today's dialogue around women on boards has nothing to do with something that happened almost 100 years ago. 'There you go again, Richard, making something out of nothing,' is what they'll say."

"And my answer to them is this: if the right to vote is worth nothing, then what was all that struggle for? The right to vote in national elections is more important than the right of owners to vote as shareholders. Or are they just different facets of the same fundamental right to express a point of view and have it count? These rights should be balanced in society and not given to one group only.

"The right to a fulfilling career is something that matters, all humans aspire, not just men, and failure to permit women to exercise this right to pursue a career is as important as the right to vote to a free society as a whole. Yes, we've move 100 years forward but that 'apartheid' that existed then still exists today on boards, on executive committees, in business circles, and in social clubs.

"Young men need to understand this, otherwise they have no context for why things are the way they are and why they need to be involved in working to change them."

WOMEN JOINING BUSINESS CLUBS

Let's start with a quotation from Peter C. Newman's book *Titans*:

> An equally serious problem was the discrimination against women as club members. Until recently, most clubs treated women with as much grace as your average Islamic state. They were barred from entry, except at Saturday afternoon weddings of members' sons and daughters when nobody else was using the facilities, or they were admitted for dinner through side doors with their husbands before art auctions. Even when allowed inside to use their cordoned off facilities, they were treated as backstairs creatures, permitted to appear only under cover of darkness, entering through separate doors into segregated quarters.[2]

Business clubs are institutions designed to demonstrate their members' success. They show that you have made it to a position that matters and you are important, just like the other members.

Exclusion means you have not made it, you are not like us, and we cannot possibly have you as part of our club. When the men on the executive committee head off to the club for lunch with the esteemed client, where is the only woman executive on the team to go? It was men only in these clubs for generations.

This is a wrong that was generally righted twenty-five years ago in the 1990s. Remember the 1990s? Well, actually, the wrong was not completely righted in the 1990s. Augusta National, in Augusta, Georgia, United States just opened up their course to women members in 2012, and the Royal and Ancient Golf of St. Andrews in St. Andrews, Scotland just opened up its membership to women in 2014. There's more.

Harvard's 225-year-old Porcellian Club, founded in 1891, spoke out publicly for the first time in April 2016, giving a controversial reason for continuing to deny women to join their exclusive ranks. This elite all-male club said they will not break from excluding women because it would make sexual assault more likely.[3]

That statement came after the Harvard University released a report that found 47 percent of female students who participated in events hosted by the Porcellian Club experienced "nonconsensual sexual contact" at some point during their time in school.

A club spokesman went on to say that forcing single gender organizations to accept members of the opposite sex could potentially increase, not decrease the potential for sexual misconduct.

"Barbara, I think that should go down as one of the greatest dodges of all time. Exclusion implies difference, and not in a positive way. Women's long periods of exclusion from places that matter have had both a societal impact and a personal impact. That impact has been on both women and men. Men come to see their relationship with women as part of the way of life, unchanging and defined by Mother Nature. It always starts with the superior place in society of men.

"Centuries of this kind of relationship cannot be undone by a few decades of a new relationship. This situation will continue until overt action by both women and men to change perspectives and behaviors overcomes what most of their grandparents thought was the way things should be."

CULTURES CLINGING TO TRADITION

"It's still very prevalent in business today, Richard, cultures clinging to tradition. Let me give you an example.

"I know a very successful woman executive who lives in Milan, Italy—we'll call her 'Isabella.' Every business quarter, Isabella leaves her office in Milan to spend a week at her investment company's headquarters in Tokyo, Japan.

"During her five years with the company, Isabella has been very successful in making profitable investments throughout Europe and was recently promoted to regional senior executive. This was a unique achievement for a woman working for a Japanese company, seeing as how Japan—at 7 percent— is the lowest is the world for women as a percentage of senior management.[4]

"Regardless of her performance and title, Isabella has never been invited to attend a business social event during any of her twenty or so weeklong visits to Tokyo. Spending evenings alone in her hotel room only punctuates her sense of aloneness and reminds her that she'll never truly be a part of the company's executive team. Because of this feeling of exclusion, Isabella is now contemplating leaving the organization.

"Not being invited to business social events while in Japan is just a reality of the Japanese male culture. Japanese men are customarily uneasy having women attend their events. Though Japan is a very advanced country in business, science, and technology, much of its culture still clings to the traditional roles of men and women. This is becoming an increasingly challenging issue in Japan, for the participation of Japanese women in business is rapidly changing as a matter of economic necessity.

"An article in the Wall Street Journal in November, 2015, noted that there is a significant shortfall of talent in Japan, from software engineers to waiters, caused by an aging workforce and education gaps. The article goes on to say that it's stunting economic growth in Japan.[5]

"What the article fails to mention is that half its population, the women, are the greatest underutilized resource in that country."

THE ASCENT OF WOMEN

Up until the 1970s, men were overrepresented in higher education, but that trend has been undergoing significant change on a global basis for thirty years now. In the 1990s, in many parts of the world, women as students began switching places with men as the dominant gender in terms of higher education. When you think about it, women have covered a lot of ground in a relatively short period of time.

There are some interesting dynamics taking place all over the globe:[6]

- In Korea, 47 percent of the student population in 2012 was composed of women, but the college entrance rate was 74 percent for women versus 68 percent for men. And among 25- to 34-year-olds in 2012, 67 percent of women had graduated from university versus 60 percent for men.
- In China and India, men still outnumber women in higher education, but the gap is closing: women make up 48 percent of the university population in China and 42 percent in India.
- And in Algeria, Bahrain, Jordan, Kuwait, Lebanon, Morocco, Oman, Qatar, Saudi Arabia, Syria, Tunisia, and the United Arab Emirates, more women than men are enrolled in university.
- In the UK, 33 percent more women than men applied for a place at university in 2014.
- In Canada, 59 percent of undergraduates are women, and women's overrepresentation is happening in almost every discipline including medicine (59 percent) and law (53 percent), with the exception of engineering, computer science, and the physical sciences.
- In the United States, nearly 60 percent of university graduates are women, plus 60 percent of master's degrees and 52 percent of doctoral degrees are awarded to women. Women broke the 50 percent mark in the attainment of PhDs in 2009 and haven't looked back since.[7]

The following chart (Figure 4.1) is taken from the last full-year study from the United States' National Center for Education Statistics. As the graph shows, women have been participating in university education to a greater degree than men since 1990.[8]

While the preceding graph applies to undergraduate studies, the statistics for graduate-level studies are consistent with these findings. Figure 4.2 indicates that, in the United States, women represented slightly more than 58 percent of those enrolled in graduate studies.

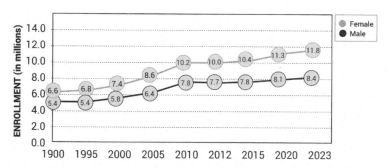

Figure 4.1 Trends in Undergraduate Enrollment by Gender, 1990–2023

	1990	2010	2020
United States	56%	58%	61%
Canada	53%	56%	62%
Brazil	53%	56%	
Peru	39%	51%	
Mexico	47%	50%	52%
Chile	46%	50%	
Argentina	46%	50%	

Figure 4.2 Women as a Percentage of University Graduates—Americas and Canada

That number is expected to rise slightly to 60 percent in 2023. That slight percentage increase is not trivial in terms of numbers of women students. The growth will be close to half a million more women in graduate schools in ten years' time compared to today.[9]

In college, women receive better grades than men do, study harder, party less, and take advantage of more educational opportunities, including corporate internships. Although better grades do not necessarily correlate with better business performance, the drive and intelligence that creates better grades does.

A 2014 Credit Suisse report, "The CS Gender 3000: Women in Senior Management," takes statistics from a database of three thousand companies from forty countries and all major industries. Their first report came out in 2012, with a more comprehensive report issued in 2014. One chart from their report (see Figure 4.3), on women's choices in higher education, is especially fascinating.[10]

On the basis of U.S. and UK data for 2011 and 2012, we can see that women represented the majority of students in medicine/dentistry, law, social science, and creative arts. Women were also within a few percentage points of representing half of all students in business, physical sciences, and mathematics.

Education Across the Globe

Although it's generally known that in the United States, Canada, and countries in Europe, women have outnumbered men in the attainment of college degrees since 1990, it is less well known that the same is true in many developing nations.

Across the globe, women complete more years of schooling than men and a higher percentage of women are attending colleges and universities than men. Here are examples of those statistics in the Americas and Canada (Figure 4.3); Europe (Figure 4.4); Eastern Europe, Middle East, and Africa (Figure 4.5); and Asia and Pacific (Figure 4.6).[11]

	UK	USA
Medicine & Dentistry	57%	48%
Physical Sciences	43%	40%
Math	42%	43%
Computer Science	16%	18%
Engineering	15%	17%
All STEM Degrees	50%	50%
Law	64%	70%
Social Sciences	60%	40%
Economics	30%	30%
Creative Arts	62%	61%
Business & Admin	51%	48%
All Degrees	57%	57%

Figure 4.3   Women as Percentage of Graduates, by Discipline

	1990	2010	2020*
Norway	55%	61%	61%
Sweden	55%	60%	63%
Denmark	55%	58%	59%
United Kingdom	51%	57%	68%
France	55%	56%	57%
Italy	53%	56%	57%
Finland	53%	54%	53%
Spain	53%	54%	55%
Germany	45%	52%	56%
Greece	48%	50%	53%

Figure 4.4   Women as a Percentage of University Graduates—Europe

	1990	2010	2020*
United Arab Emirates	N/A	60%	
Poland	57%	58%	58%
Hungary	53%	58%	60%
Russia	56%	57%	
Israel	N/A	56%	
Saudi Arabia	47%	55%	
Iran	36%	51%	
Turkey	38%	43%	43%
Egypt	N/A	43%	
Iraq	N/A	36%	
Central African Republic	15%	31%	

Figure 4.5 Women as a Percentage of University Graduates—Eastern Europe, Middle East, and Africa

	1990	2010	2020*
New Zealand	56%	58%	60%
Australia	51%	55%	55%
Philippines	NA	54%	
Hong Kong	43%	51%	
Mainland China	NA	49%	
Malaysia	NA	49%	
Vietnam	NA	48%	
Japan	44%	46%	47%
India	36%	39%	
South Korea	37%	38%	39%

Figure 4.6 Women as a Percentage of University Graduates—Asia and Pacific

"It's amazing, Richard, how women are dominating higher education and have been for so long now. What's equally surprising is that the gap between women's higher education and their positions in leadership hasn't closed accordingly, and this is a huge blind spot for organizations pursuing new talent now and for the years to come.

"Women are pursuing college and advanced degrees for a reason and the safest thing to assume is that all of our assumptions are outdated when it comes to ambition in pursuing careers—whether that's in Japan, Saudi Arabia, or Chile. Many who consider themselves wired in and on top of all the important trends are still missing this one in a huge way, and to their economic disadvantage."

Under My Very Nose!

Let me share with you a recent exchange I had with a client of mine, a senior executive in his early forties in the financial services industry in the United States.

Halfway through our discussion about women as financial advisors, he said, "Barbara, to be honest with you, I'm always uneasy about hiring women. They're not in it for the duration and family always seems to come first. There are about eight women I know in our circle of friends in our own neighborhood who are home now and not working. Most of them have master's degrees, in a variety of fields."

I asked him, "Do you know why they're home? Have you asked?"

"No," he said, "I just assumed that there were family reasons. All of them are in their early thirties. That means their focus is on parenthood."

I suggested he try an experiment and conduct an informal focus group with the eight women and ask them about their situations. He discovered that, in every single instance, each woman left the company she was working for because she didn't feel valued and wasn't engaged in the work. Each enthusiastically wanted to find another job or even a new career but they were generally uncertain how to go about landing a job with a company with which they would want to belong. Many felt discouraged.

A short time after the focus group, he hired six of the eight women and trained them as financial service advisors and each is doing a spectacular job building her book of business. He realized how dated his assumptions really were and was amazed that he found that talent under his very nose in his own neighborhood!

Positive Global Signals

So what will a world with 60 percent of graduates being female look like? Certainly not the same as it looks today. The proportion of women running companies globally has risen to nearly 12 percent in 2014 up from just 5 percent in 2012. Here are some other significant findings:[12]

- Economies in Eastern Europe (37 percent) and Southeast Asia (35 percent) are leading the way on women in leadership.
- In China, 63 percent of companies have a woman CFO.
- In Russia, 43 percent of businesses have women in senior management (the highest percentage anywhere in the world).
- In Latin America, 40 percent of businesses have no women in senior management, but in two of the continent's fastest growing economies—Peru (35 percent) and Chile (30 percent)—women hold relatively high percentages of senior management positions.
- In Africa, where great strides have been made to increase female participation in politics, both Botswana (32 percent) and South Africa (26 percent) rank above the global average for women in senior management.

This tells us that many of the global signals are very positive for women and that these signals have been improving for some time. Perhaps some gains in the developed world are slowing, but this comes after a period of rapid growth. With the number of women at universities in undergraduate and graduate programs rising dramatically, we will see further participation by women at all levels of corporate life.

AN ECONOMIC NECESSITY VERSUS A CHOICE

"Nevertheless, Richard, progress is far too slow when you consider the tsunami of women with graduate degrees looking for jobs and advancement. Since the 1980s, in parallel with all the global statistics we just saw on education, industrialized nations have experienced major changes in the steady increase of women's participation in the paid workforce. In the United States, 72 percent of all women between 25 and 54 are employed and 59 percent of women of that age group are employed in the European Union.[13]

"The dynamic that's driving this steady and irreversible increase in women entering business is more an economic necessity than anything.

"We're still talking as if it's a freedom now or a choice for women to work. The reality since the 1980s is that it's an economic necessity for women to work and for families to have dual career couples. It's an economic necessity for women to work for the benefit of society."

"The International Monetary Fund estimates that there is plenty of evidence that when women are able to develop their full labor market potential, there can be significant economic gains for societies. Their studies, Barbara, suggest that raising the female labor force participation rate to country-specific male levels would, for instance, raise the GDP in the United States by 5 percent, in Japan by 9 percent, in the United Arab Emirates by 12 percent, and in Egypt by 34 percent."[14]

"Richard, if I had a choice, there were many years in my career that I would not have worked. The reality is that 99 percent have to work to make ends meet, and maybe 1 percent can choose not to work. That 1 percent is made up of senior male leaders who just don't understand the economic necessity of it all. Let me give you an example.

"I recently met with a client who happens to be a male executive vice president who has a woman on his team who wants to be a vice president. She's done a pretty good job in her director role but doesn't have a big portfolio of accomplishments. He doesn't believe she's ready for the VP level, but he tells me she keeps applying, even though he keeps telling her that she's not ready yet. He then shared that she's Indian, thirty-five, and single. She was top of her MBA class.

"I said to him, 'Have you asked her why she's pushing for this?'

"He replied, 'I think she's overly ambitious. She was at the top of her MBA class and is probably getting pressure from the family because she's still single. So she's just over-compensating and overachieving.'

"I said, 'Maybe not, that's your assumption. Why don't you ask her?'

"And he did, he asked her. He discovered that she's providing income for her entire family: both parents and grandparents, and for herself and her brother. So she's striving to bring in more income, not for self-serving reasons. She probably aced her way through her MBA courses so she could become the breadwinner for the family."

AREAS WHERE GLASS CEILINGS STILL EXIST

There are five disciplines where women are clearly not benefiting from their college degrees. Two of them, medicine and law, have been dominated by women in education, particularly in the United States, for over thirty years now.

The other two areas are engineering and computer science, two of the fastest growing fields for well-paying jobs, yet fewer women are seeking those degrees now than they have in the past. And finally, in finance, women have dominated advanced degrees in business for over thirty years as well as entry level and mid-level management, but are still hard to find at the top of the house. Let's first look into medicine and law.

Women in Medicine

No product we can think of that both women and men purchase is more heavily influenced by women than health care. Every family has someone driving these critical decisions, and the vast majority of the time that person is the mother, wife, sister, or aunt. Biologically, females are the nurturers and the caregiving role is more natural to women.

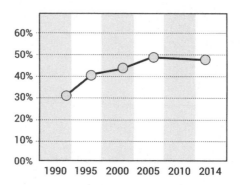

Figure 4.7   Percentage of Medical Degrees Attained by Women, 1990–2014

It stands to reason that young women would be interested in an education in medicine and be more adept at making critical decisions in the field of health care. So yes, women have attained over a third of the medical degrees (MDs) earned in the United States since the 1990s and nearly half since the 2000s (see Figure 4.7).[15]

Yet, despite representing nearly 50 percent of medical doctors, and despite making up more than 73 percent of the health care workforce, women today represent only 21 percent of executives and 17 percent of board members at Fortune 500 health care companies. Of the 125 women who carry an executive title, only five serve in operating roles as COO or president. And there's only one women CEO of a Fortune 500 health care company.[16]

In a survey of over four hundred women in the health care industry by RockHealth released in February, 2015, 96 percent of the women surveyed believe that gender discrimination still exists in the medical profession. And 45 percent cite gender as one of the biggest hurdles they've faced professionally.[17]

Many of these barriers that surface out of cultural assumptions and antiquated attitudes and practices put women at a disadvantage. Unfortunately, fewer women leaders mean fewer role models for the young women attaining degrees in order to practice medicine, and for many, to be leaders in the medical profession and ultimately influence the direction of health care.

Women in Law

Considering the fact that women have received nearly half of the law degrees conferred in the United States since 1990, there's been very little cumulative growth in the percentage of women as partners (see Figure 4.8).[18]

Once they receive their degrees, women attorneys are not entering or staying with law firms. If they do join a law firm, they're leaving after one or two years to start their own practice. In a broad study following the careers of men and women law graduates of Columbia, Harvard, Berkeley, Michigan, and Yale,

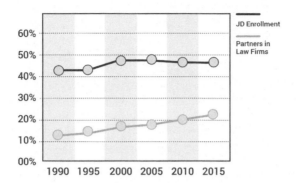

Figure 4.8 Women as a Percentage of JD Enrollment and as Partners in Law Firms, 1990–2015

the women believed that women lawyers experienced significant barriers to their careers because of a lack of mentoring and exclusion from informal networks within their law firms.

Aside from being nearly equally enrolled in law schools, women work alongside men as associates in law firms in equal numbers with men. Yet, women are twice as likely as men to leave law firms. In a survey of over seventeen thousand law firm associates, women rated their firms' culture, their job satisfaction, and their compensation much lower than male associates did. All of this may shed some light on the statistic that only 4 percent of the top two hundred U.S. law firms have female, firm-wide managing partners.[19]

Women in Engineering

For the past two decades, 20 percent of engineering graduates have been women (see Figure 4.9), yet only 11 percent of practicing engineers are women. Compared with other skilled professions such as accounting, medicine, and law, engineering has the highest turnover of women.

Although there are many programs in place at undergraduate universities to feed the engineering pipeline, when women graduate and enter the workforce, that's when they face the problems that ultimately cause them to leave engineering.[20, 21, 22]

Conventional wisdom says that women in engineering face obstacles such as the glass ceiling, a lack of self-confidence, and a lack of mentors. But psychologists who delved deeper into the issue with a new study found that the biggest pushbacks female engineers receive come from the environments they work in.

A survey was taken of fifty-three hundred women who earned engineering degrees in the United States over the past six decades in order to determine why so few women stayed in engineering. Only 62 percent were currently working in

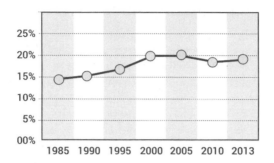

Figure 4.9   Percentage of Bachelor's Degrees in Engineering Awarded to Women,
1985–2013

engineering, and 38 percent had either left the profession or never entered the
field to begin with. Here are some of the reasons they provided:[23]

- An "old-boys club" still exists in many engineering organizations with many
  calling the engineering workplace unfriendly and even hostile to women.
  It's interesting that many of these "old boys" are members of generation X
  and even the millennial generation.
- There is no opportunity for advancement in a male-dominated field. The
  culture of engineering is male-centric with high expectations for travel and
  little personal time.
- There isn't a strong network of females in engineering. You either become
  one of the guys or blaze your own trail, which is very difficult.
- Lack of confidence was not a factor as to why women left engineering—the
  study found no difference in confidence levels between those who left or
  stayed in the field.
- Only 17 percent left engineering because of caregiving reasons, which
  dispels the notion that pregnancy plays a big part in keeping women out.
  Many who did leave for parenthood, though, did so because their companies didn't offer flexible enough work-life policies.
- The women who stay in engineering do so because they want to ensure that
  they are making a difference.

The study found that women's sentiments didn't differ between engineering
disciplines. Women faced the same issues in the fields of aerospace, biotech, and
computer science.

Always on Call

"Richard, we mentioned wake-up calls in Chapter 1, but here's a wake-up that
a CEO I know had that changed his entire engineering firm, a highly revered
engineering company that had its origins back in the 1960s.

"He recently lost two top women engineers, and the CEO realized that the culture they had established over sixty years ago was driving women out the door, as well as younger men. 'On call 24/7' was the mantra of the baby boomer men who defined the work ethic and positioning of the engineering firm all those years ago and it was driving away very talented women engineers.

"It was a wake-up call for him because he couldn't afford to lose that talent. The CEO implemented a part-time worker program where engineers could work 75 percent of the time rather than full time.

"They tried it out and it worked brilliantly and they now have the best retention rate of any engineering company and are attracting the best talent. It has hurt women a bit in terms of advancing, but it's been a huge differentiator for them."

Women in Computer Science

Before 1970, women earned between 10 and 15 percent of computer science bachelor's degrees. By the early 1980s, the number rose to 37 percent. However, the trend began to reverse in 1985 (see Figure 4.10), an astounding rate of decline in a high-demand field of study and booming technological future.[24]

In 2013, 18 percent of bachelor's degrees in computing were earned by women.[25] Part of this decline is because computer science has become, in many ways, a male-identified field—an identity that's even played out in television and film. During the 1990s, hiring practices also began to favor men, according to a recent study by the American Association of University Women (AAUW) that cites the creation of professional organizations, networks, and hierarchies that supported the entry of men into the field and tended to push women out.

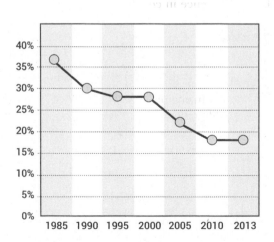

Figure 4.10 Percentage of Bachelor's Degrees in Computer Science Awarded to Women, 1985–2013

The study also points out that once employed in computer science, women are more likely to leave than men. They tend to suffer from isolation.[26]

Although women have reached senior positions at Facebook, Xerox, IBM, Oracle, and other large companies, they're absent at the top of many IT departments. Women are underrepresented in STEM for reasons that tend to discourage participation:[27]

- A lack of role models and mentors at the top
- STEM careers not welcome areas for women to work in (entry level and middle-management)
- Preconceived notion that women have other priorities, as in starting a family
- Lack of role models and mentors in high school and college
- Sexism in schools and cultural stigma against girls entering STEM before high school

Computer science is an increasingly popular major due to growing interest in social media (of which women are greater users than men), prevalence of computers in everyday life, higher-paying job opportunities, and the perception of a more stable career.

The AAUW study indicates that as much as 80 percent of the new jobs in STEM are computing jobs, and they typically require only a bachelor's degree and not a master's degree as in the other sciences.[28]

Since the 1980s, computer science has become a much more vital doorway to high-paying jobs and satisfying careers for techies that offer the chance to innovate and influence the software-driven future of society. Yet far and away more men than women are stepping through that doorway.

Women in Finance

For over thirty years, women have had high representation in disciplines of study, such as accounting, finance, and business administration, that tend to flow into the fields of finance and financial services. As illustrated in Figure 4.11, the 1980s, women have received half of the bachelor's degrees in business administration and in recent years have climbed to earn nearly half of all MBAs awarded in the United States.[29]

For equally as many years, women have filled entry-level positions in finance and today represent 63 percent of all accounting and auditing positions in the United States, 53 percent of financial managers, and 41 percent of financial analysts.[30]

In Canada, women's professional representation at entry- and mid-level positions in business and finance has also been prominent (and dominant in many instances) for an equally long period of time. They represent 55 percent of financial managers; 44 percent of insurance, real estate, and financial brokerage

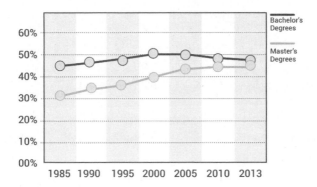

Figure 4.11   Percentage of Bachelor's and Master's Degrees in Business Awarded to Women, 1985–2013

managers; 57 percent of banking, credit, and other investment managers; and 51 percent of financial and investment analysts.[31]

Even globally, as shown in Figure 4.12, women today represent nearly half of all employees in the global financial services industry:[32]

Finland	60.9%
France	57.6%
Germany	51.2%
Italy	45.4%
Japan	51.8%
Mexico	49.9%
Norway	52.5%
Portugal	45.6%
Spain	48.1%
Sweden	51.1%
Switzerland	39.8%
United Kingdom	43.7%

Figure 4.12   Women as a Percentage of Employees in the Global Financial Services Industry

CEOs	2.1%
Board Seats	18.7%
Executive / Senior-Level Officers and Managers	29.3%
First / Mid-Level Officers and Managers	46.1%
Industry Labor Force	54.3%

Figure 4.13 Percentage of Women in Finance in the S&P 500, 2014

Yet, in every sector of the financial services industry, the higher up the ladder the lower the percentage of women in leadership positions (Figure 4.13). We see this in the percentage of women in finance in the S&P 500:[33]

Meanwhile, almost all the studies since the 1990s by McKinsey & Company, Catalyst, Credit Suisse, and dozens of others have unequivocally shown that increasing the percentage of women in senior management and on corporate boards improves the financial performance of companies.

There have long been concerns about the lack of women at senior levels in financial services. Many have suggested that the extreme risk taking and neglect of clients and customers that led to the recession of 2008 were caused by the overwhelming masculinity at the decision-making level of the industry. The cost to the industry is even greater than that.

According to recent research from the Center for Talent Innovation (CTI), the financial services industry is a perfect example of a sector that risks missing trillions of dollars in potential business in the United States alone, simply because its professionals don't exemplify the behaviors needed and its firms haven't built the cultures required to access the female market.

Women create, control, and influence an enormous amount of wealth around the world. In the United States alone, women exercise decision-making power over $11.2 trillion—that's 39 percent of the nation's investable assets. Yet this dynamic and growing market is amazingly unused and unacknowledged by the industry that serves it.[34]

ENDNOTES

1. "Women's Suffrage: When and Where Did Women Earn the Right to Vote?" © 2000–2017, Sandbox Networks, Inc., publishing as Infoplease, http://www .infoplease.com/ipa/A0931343.html.

2. Peter C. Newman, "Titans: How the Canadian Establishment Seized Power" (New York: Viking Press, October 29, 1998).

3. Laura Bult, "Harvard's All-Male Porcellian Club Defends 225-Year Exclusion of Women Saying Admitting Female Students Would Increase 'Sexual Misconduct,'" *New York Daily News*, April 13, 2016, http://www.nydailynews.com/news/national/harvard-club-admitting-women-increase-sex-assault-article-1.2600012.

4. Catalyst, *Quick Take: Women in Management, Global Comparison* (New York: Catalyst, 2014), http://www.catalyst.org/knowledge/women-management-global-comparison.

5. Alexander Martin, "Lack of Workers Hobbles Japan's Growth," *Wall Street Journal*, November 15, 2015, http://www.wsj.com/articles/lack-of-workers-hobbles-japans-growth-1447635365.

6. Stephan Vincent-Lancrin, "The Reversal of Gender Inequalities in Higher Education: An Ongoing Trend," OECD (Organization for Economic Cooperation and Development) Report, October 2014, Vol. 1, Chapter 10, http://www.oecd.org/edu/ceri/41939699.pdf.

7. Daniel de Vise, "More Women Than Men Got PhDs Last Year," *The Washington Post*, September 14, 2010, http://www.washingtonpost.com/wp-dyn/content/article/2010/09/13/AR2010091306555.html.

8. NCES (National Center for Education Statistics), "Digest of Education Statistics, Actual and Projected Undergraduate Enrollment in Degree-Granting Postsecondary Institutions, by Sex: Fall 1990–2023." https://nces.ed.gov/programs/coe/indicator_cha.asp.

9. NCES (National Center for Education Statistics), "Digest of Education Statistics: Enrollment in Educational Institutions, by Level and Control of Institution, Enrollment Level, and Attendance Status and Sex of Student, Fall 1990–2023." https://nces.ed.gov/programs/digest/d13/tables/dt13_105.20.asp.

10. Credit Suisse "The CS Gender 3000, Women in Senior Management," September, 2014, 9, https://publications.credit-suisse.com/tasks/render/file/index.cfm?fileid=8128F3C0-99BC-22E6-838E2A5B1E4366DF.

11. UNESCO Institute for Statistics, "Percent of Women in Education, 2011, and United Nations 2020 Projections," Organization for Economic Cooperation and Development, 2014, http://unstats.un.org/unsd/demographic/products/worldswomen/Gender%20statistics%20sources.htm.

12. Grant Thornton International Business Report, 2014, "Women in Business: The Path to Leadership," https://www.grantthornton.global/en/insights/articles/women-in-business-2015/

13. Andrea E. Abele and Judith Volmer, "Dual-Career Couples: Specific Challenges for Work-Life Integration," *Research Gate*, January 2011, 180–181, https://www.researchgate.net/publication/226134388_Dual-Career_Couples_Specific_Challenges_for_Work-Life_Integration.

14. Katrin Elborgh-Woytek, Monique Newiak, Kalpana Kochhar, Stefania Fabrizio, Kangni Kpodar, Philippe Wingender, Benedict Clements, and Gerd Schwartz, "Women, Work, and the Economy: Macroeconomic Gains from Gender Equity," https://www.imf.org/external/pubs/ft/sdn/2013/sdn1310.pdf.

15. The Association of American Medical Colleges, "Medical Students, Selected Years, 1965–2013," July, 2014, Table 1, https://www.aamc.org/download/411782/data/2014_table1.pdf.

16. Halle Tecco, "The State of Women in Healthcare: An Update," *Rock-Health*, March 23, 2015, https://rockhealth.com/state-women-healthcare update/.

17. Ibid.

18. Catalyst Knowledge Center, "Women in Law in Canada and the U.S.," Catalyst Research, March 3, 2015, http://www.catalyst.org/knowledge/women-law-canada-and-us.

19. Selena Rezvani, "Large Law Firms Are Failing Women Lawyers," *The Washington Post*, February 18, 2014, https://www.washingtonpost.com/news/on-leadership/wp/2014/02/18/large-law-firms-are-failing-women-lawyers/.

20. National Science Foundation, "Women, Minorities, and Persons with Disabilities in Science and Engineering: Bachelor's Degrees Awarded, by Sex and Field: 2002–2012," https://www.nsf.gov/statistics/2017/nsf17310/static/data/tab2-4.pdf.

21. National Center for Education Statistics, "Digest of Education Statistics: Bachelor's Degrees Awarded, by Sex and Field: 1990–1998," https://nces.ed.gov/programs/digest/d13/tables/dt13_322.20.asp.

22. Susan T. Hill, "Science and Engineering Bachelor's Degrees Awarded to Women Increase Overall, but Decline in Several Fields," National Science Foundation, *NSF 97-326*, November 7, 1997, http://www.nsf.gov/statistics/databrf/sdb97326.htm.

23. Nicolas St. Fleur, "Many Women Leave Engineering, Blame the Work Culture," NPR, *All Tech Considered*, August 12, 2014, http://www.npr.org/sections/alltechconsidered/2014/08/12/339638726/many-women-leave-engineering-blame-the-work-culture.

24. National Center for Education Statistics, "Degrees in Computer and Information Sciences Conferred by Degree-Granting Institutions, by Level of Degree and Sex of Student: 1970–71 through 2010–11," https://nces.ed.gov/programs/digest/d12/tables/dt12_349.asp.

25. Erik Sherman, "Report: Disturbing Drop in Women in Computing Field," *Fortune*, March 26, 2015, http://fortune.com/2015/03/26/report-the-number-of-women-entering-computing-took-a-nosedive/.

26. Catherine Hill, "Solving the Equation: The Variables for Women's Success in Engineering and Computing," American Association of University Women, http://www.aauw.org/research/solving-the-equation/.

27. Ibid.

28. Ibid.

29. National Center for Educational Statistics, "Degrees in Business Conferred by Postsecondary Institutions, by Level of Degree and Sex of Student: Selected Years, 1955–56 through 2012–13," https://nces.ed.gov/programs/digest/d14/tables/dt14_325.25.asp.

30. Catalyst Knowledge Center, "Women in Canadian, US, and Global Financial Services," Catalyst Research, December 2, 2015, http://www.catalyst.org/knowledge/women-canadian-us-and-global-financial-services.

31. Ibid.

32. Ibid.

33. Ibid.

34. Sylvia Ann Hewlett and Andrea Turner Moffitt with Melinda Marshall, "Harnessing the Power of the Purse: Female Investors and Global Opportunities for Growth," Center for Talent Innovation, May 2014, http://www.talentinnovation.org/_private/assets/HarnessingThePowerOfThePurse_ExecSumm-CTI-CONFIDENTIAL.pdf.

Chapter 5

ASCENT OF MEN

The leaders of most businesses today are men. There is no question that men have built amazing corporations, achieved tremendous feats of production, developed new technologies in agriculture and consumer products, and globalized the world, thereby lifting millions out of poverty across the globe. These achievements have resulted in the wealth of the world increasing nearly continuously for centuries.

Of course many women also played important roles, but it took societal change to begin to realize their potential and that progress has been slow. The purpose of *Results at the Top* is to convince these same leaders that their organizations would function and perform even better if they combined the talents of women and men in order to lead their organizations into the future.

MEN ACCELERATING CHANGE

Men have played important roles in all of the significant developments involving bringing women into positions where they can achieve the full realization of their potential. Men were the ones who created the legislation to give women the right to vote and it was men who voted in favor of that legislation. How do we know? Why of course it was men, because women had no right to vote at that time.

How about the millions of men who supported the Equal Rights Amendment in the United States? No, it did not succeed, but that does not diminish all of the support that men provided in the effort.

How about the business clubs that have voted to end the decades-long process of excluding women? Of course it was men who made these changes.

Today we have many men who are committed to the concept that women are able to lead in any capacity and that bringing more women into leadership roles will improve their organization. We are seeing this change play out right in front of us. That does not mean that progress has not been slower than many would like; however, if we can increase the number of men who think like Warren Buffett, change will accelerate and we will all see the benefits.

Listen to the "Sage of Omaha" during a BBC interview in 2013. Here is a man who gets it and whose perspective, as he is regarded as one of the greatest business minds and investors of our time, carries weight and influence. Buffett commented on the vast potential with women in leadership with men:

> Women have been subjugated for time immemorial. I saw it in my own family. I was born in 1930 with an older sister and a younger sister, and the hope was that they would marry well and the hope for me was that I would fulfill my potential, whatever that would be.
>
> They were two human beings with enormous potential and it was assumed they could be a nurse or a secretary or a flight attendant. Or they could be a teacher—but not in upper education.
>
> What a waste of human talent—50 percent of the population was pushed off into the corner for 200 years. I see how far we've come using only half the talent in the country and now we're getting to the point that we are using 100 percent. It makes me optimistic but we still have a ways to go.[1]

There are increasingly more men who do get it and others such as Warren Buffett who are acting on it. Yet, as we look across the landscape today and in our nearly thirty years of experience with leadership in companies across the globe, we can generally place male leaders into one of three types or groupings when it comes to men's attitudes toward advancing women in leadership, which we explore in the following sections.[2]

Those Who Get It and Are Acting on It

There are male leaders today who get it and are acting on it. Their stories dot this chapter and are found throughout this book. When leaders become aware of the economic power of men and women leading together—most especially when they see the results of women in leadership—their mindset changes, the culture shifts, and the organization as a whole begins to behave more productively and effectively. You know who these leaders are by their statements:

- "We publicly support, endorse, and act on gender diversity."
- "We publicize our diversity progress frequently and at all levels."
- "Our firm is stronger for having including women at all levels of leadership."
- "We intend to hire more women in key positions for it improves our firm's innovativeness and productivity."

Those Who Believe in It but Don't Know What to Do

Believers recognize the value of women in leadership but don't know what to do or even realize that they need to be involved. They're comfortable in their environment. They don't realize that nothing will change unless they themselves act on it. These male leaders are in organizations whose leadership still doesn't view gender diversity as a strategic imperative, and diversity efforts often give way to other priorities. Here is how you know who these leaders are:

- "I have some excellent women on my team but I wish I could find more."
- "I wish I knew what women want from me in my business."
- "I am really busy but I support what HR is doing to promote gender diversity."
- "If only more women applied for jobs, I would give them more jobs."
- "I support women, but I really worry that my male staff members will not accept women in certain roles. I still have to keep the place going."

Those Who Don't Get It or Don't Care to

The men in this category are generally not interested in the subject of women in leadership. They don't see it as part of their critical path. Their focus is on other priorities and they generally treat gender diversity as an annoyance and a nonissue, often to their own detriment. Unfortunately, a large number of male leaders share this mindset, but not as large a number as the men who believe and want to see change. Here are some typical statements by the male leaders in this category:

- "We just cannot find enough qualified female candidates."
- "No women applied for the roles."
- "We just do not know why women leave our firm."
- "Women are not part of our industry and cannot understand what we do."
- "We have many other priorities besides advancing women."

Based on our work with many male executives over the years, the following chart (Figure 5.1), though not scientific, fairly accurately represents the distribution of men's stances—particularly in the Western world—on the advancement of women. If we were to estimate men's attitudes globally, the percentage of those who get it and are actively involved in the advancement of women would be undervalued. There has been progress in the West though, and that is what is reflected in these percentages as well.

Our goal with *Results at the Top* is to move the men in the middle bar to the left (see Figure 5.2) and into the group who get it and are actively involved. The men who don't get it will begin to fade into the background at an accelerating rate in the next several years.

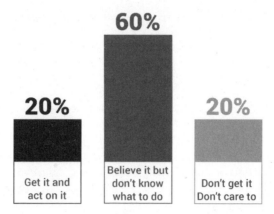

Figure 5.1 Three Types of Male Leaders and Their Attitudes Toward Advancing Women in Leadership

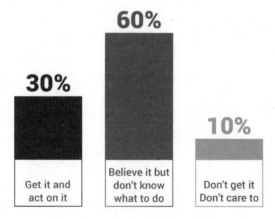

Figure 5.2 Ten Percent More Male Leaders Who Get It and Are Acting on It

Every person in a social system, just as every male leader in business, does not adopt innovative ideas, new products, or new practices at the same time. Diffusion research suggests that instead, people tend to adopt in a time sequence. Diffusion theory also says that adoption of a new idea can only happen through human interaction and the sharing of knowledge. [3]

If a male leader who has experienced the value of women in leadership in his organization discusses it with two other male leaders of two completely different companies, and these two become adopters who pass the knowledge along to two other colleagues in other companies, and so on, the trend will begin spread geometrically.

The "tipping point" for a movement to catch fire is when the critical mass of early adopters reaches 13.5 percent.[4] Of course, time is the unknown element, but we're not waiting another two hundred years for change to come in the advancement of women into leadership with men. If we want to accelerate time, we have to change the percentages drastically.

Imagine the global impact if just 10 percent more men became actively involved in creating gender-diverse leadership teams. We believe we're at that tipping point now. Knowledge will motivate increasingly more male believers in the middle to join the ranks of those who are actively involved. We could change the world!

THE EVOLUTION OF AN ATTITUDE

"Barbara, I know this chapter title is following the 'Ascent,' theme in this book, but another title for this chapter could have been 'The Evolution of the Attitude of Men.' As we say earlier, men have been instrumental in supporting the accomplishments of women over the decades. Yet we know that some do not support the premise of *Gender Success* and improving leadership through gender equality. I have to tell you that the guys who are not on board yet after having read the first three chapters will, well, fade increasingly into irrelevance. They are anachronisms with attitudes long ago disproven."

"Richard, I've seen a significant change in the attitudes of men. When I first started out on this Gender Intelligence journey, the resistance and denial was much greater than it is today. Though we're certainly not where we need to be at this point, there are increasingly more men who get it. We are on the path and more men are recognizing the value of having women in leadership positions alongside men."

"We're going to hear from a few male leaders in this chapter who will share their 'Aha' moment—the point when they realized the value of women in leadership and the value of difference-thinking to decision making. But let's start with you and how you came to be such a strong and vocal advocate."

Richard's Story

Over the run of my career I have learned that including women and men in my management teams led to superior results compared to men alone (or women alone, although I rarely had that opportunity).

I did not come to this conclusion until I had substantial experience in management. In fact, I did not care much about the issue for the first half of my working life. But as I took on larger, more complex tasks, I had to seek greater diversity in the creation of the teams. Inevitably I became convinced that diversity led to better results than if I had limited myself to the narrower universe of men. I did not really know why this happened, but, much as in my understanding of many things in life—the existence of gravity, or the safety of air flight, or why left- and right-wing governments adopt identical policies once they get into office—I accepted this as a fact.

I became an advocate for this approach in the firms that I joined. My views often met with mixed reactions, but I did not care. It worked for me, and I intended to keep doing it. As I became more senior I was able to effect systemic change in the firms I served. We would hire more women graduates at the introductory level, we would have programs to hang on to these women through the critical first seven to ten years of their career, and we would move women into more senior levels to be visible role models not only to other women but also to men.

In order to get support for this approach I had to get the men I worked with on my side. Remember: today, it is men who lead most companies—which is why *Results at the Top* speaks to men about how it is in their interest to change their preconceptions and behavior.

It is unlikely to be regulation and quotas (or even this book) that will result in large-scale change to the composition of corporate management structures. As always, ultimately it will be the market that brings about sustainable change. Market forces are clearly showing us that men and women together in diverse management teams outperform traditional male-only structures. In the short run, more people need to understand the opportunity that presents itself. Adding women to senior teams is a costless way to improve corporate performance. In the long run, nothing else should be necessary for companies acting rationally and in their own interest. Men are the ones who have to see the need for acting on change. It is often men who will make the decisions to implement what is required to get done. Many men have already gotten there, some are getting themselves there, and others will fade away when they cannot get themselves to change. The inevitability of change arising from market forces is as unstoppable and as undeniable as the laws of nature.

What About Me?

Managers at all levels need to understand how employees will react to conversations you have with them. Predicting human behavior can be difficult at the best of times, and it doesn't get easier in high-stress work environments. This is one of the biggest reasons why management is so difficult and is as much of an art as a science. Fortunately, your skills should improve with experience.

However, we can describe a major element of male behavior. When you sit down with a male employee to give him news that may or may not affect him, be aware that every male has a recorded message running in the back of his head on repeat, asking the question: "What about me?"

When we first explain this to fellow managers, many of them are shocked. Even if the males among *them* flat out deny this attitude exists, deep within them they know it is true. Surely men could not be so self-centered that their reaction to everything is "What about me?" But this recording is deeply embedded in the male psyche and has been since early evolution. Many men learn to ignore it or find ways to benefit from situations that are not completely self-centered; for example, they give to charitable causes. But that does not mean that "What about me?" isn't running in the background of their brain. It is always there. And it's kind of comical.

Imagine that as a manager of ABC, you call your employees together to tell them about a new initiative called the ABC Women in Leadership Scholarship Program. The program is designed to help women advance into more senior management positions by continuing their education at university.

Given that management wants to have more diversity in their choices of new management candidates, this seems to be a logical program to put in place. However, as you describe this program to the group in front of you, composed mostly of male employees between 25 and 35, you can be sure that "What about me?" is running through their heads, and that they're still asking the question when they leave the room.

This is why it is important for all employees to be taken into account when creating a diversity solution. Management can achieve this by having comparable programs for both female and male employees. Even if some programs are targeted specifically toward women, some others can be created for men or targeted at both sexes.

There is no need to create additional tension by making men and women compete for top management's attention. An even-handed approach to employee development pays off as the organization becomes recognized for caring about all employees.

Men are made with this "What about me?" trait for good and valid reasons. My discussion of men's behavior with regard to gender diversity in business will often come back to this hardwiring. As we shall see throughout this book, women's advancement to senior management and governance positions will happen only when men embrace this as a positive answer to the "What about me?" question and move beyond this to understand that gender diversity is the best outcome for everyone, together.

Unless men make this change, women will be forced to slug it out inch-by-inch, and gender balance will be reached slowly if at all. Do women deserve better? Yes they do. But as Will Munny (Clint Eastwood) says to Big Bill (Gene Hackman) in the film *Unforgiven*: "Deserve's got nothin' to do with it."[5]

> "Barbara, one thing that every man and woman finds difficult is when their employees, their boss, a senior leader, their customers, or others begin to behave in an unacceptable way towards each other. What distinguishes most of these actions is a person with more power than another who uses that power improperly. This topic is difficult to discuss but needs to be out in the open. Here it is."

Some Men Are Out of Line!

"Ask any man in confidence what they think about the behavior of some of their fellow men and you'll learn how disgusted they are and how helpless they feel about what to do about it. Ask any business woman and you will get an earful. Almost every female executive has experienced some form of this bad actor in the workplace.

"Barbara, this is a difficult subject, but one that businesspeople struggle with and are surprised by on a regular, too frequent, basis. We are lost when it comes to overt bad behavior between men and women in the workplace or between employees outside the workplace."

"Richard, I've come across this challenge for male leaders so many times and in a variety of settings. The male code gets in the way for many men, especially when it's their boss who's showing the bad behavior. There are ways of addressing it though, and more men are stepping up and letting it be known the kind of inclusive culture they want for the company.

"It is a shocking title but a personal experience of mine earlier in my career has me agreeing with the language. Let me tell you about one of my experiences."

Barbara's Story

"It was at the onset of my career and I was excited about this role as I felt that I was being taken seriously as a professional. It was an important step in my career. I had a new wardrobe, which included some pantsuits, which women were beginning to wear in the office. I respected my boss when I first took the role. However something happened to change that.

"One day I was working in the office and my boss asked me to come into his office. I wondered what this was about. Upon entering his office he asked me a couple of questions about what I was working on and then asked me to get a book off a high shelf in his office. I did this as a courtesy and then the meeting was over.

"Well not quite. A couple of hours later he asked me to come into his office once again. OK now what? Well after pleasantries, he asked me to pick up something from the corner floor of his office. Again I did this as a courtesy; after all he was the boss. Meeting over.

"Not yet. A third time he asked me to come into his office and again wanted me to get him a book off of a high shelf. This was getting strange. So I asked him why he needed me to come into his office to get these things for him.

"His answer was, 'I just like the way you look when you leave my office.'

"What was he talking about? Did he really say that? Did this mean what I thought it meant? Unfortunately, yes it did.

"So I told him what I thought of his behavior in no uncertain terms. In the longer run I knew I could not work with this person, but I didn't have to worry about that much longer. Within a year, he was fired. I'm not sure of the reasons why. I expect that it had something to do with his behavior toward women in the office."

Is this an isolated incident or something that occurs all too frequently? Unfortunately every woman and man has her or his stories. It gets even worse when there is physical assault taking place and laws are broken. Recently the Canadian Broadcasting Corporation had an on-air personality accused of sexual assault by three women.

> Repeat after me: Just because an event was not reported in the past—that does not mean that it did not happen.

The case received intensive media coverage, it represented personal tragedy, plus the reputational damage to the employees and to the firm was substantial. It recently went to trial and the verdict was not guilty. The reasons given by the judge included that the complainants failed to give a full account of their relationship with the accused. This was understandable, given the events had occurred many years in the past. One thing we all have learned is that just because an event was not reported in the past, it does not mean that it did not happen.

How many times have we personally witnessed this in our workplace, neighborhood, or community? The victims are embarrassed or shy or intimidated. Think of the child victims of pedophiles. Think of those confronted by racism. The same process can happen. Victims are afraid to come forward for fear of embarrassment with their families and friends or that they will invite retribution from the perpetrators.

Organizations are all vulnerable to a small number of their employees harming their fellow employees and in doing so creating a toxic workplace environment and ultimately putting the entire organization at risk.

What should be done?

First of all, this is an issue where the culture of the organization must not tolerate this behavior. The tone from the CEO and other managers needs to constantly reinforce this view. Victims need to be encouraged to report these acts in a manner free from intimidation as soon as it happens.

Hotlines are rarely effective. Human resource departments can be effective only if they believe their job is the welfare of the employees and not simply to protect the firm from financial or reputational damage. Infractions need to be dealt with immediately and seriously. Failing to do so is in a way condoning the behavior. Students in business schools today are taught that it is not good enough to not participate in an improper activity. If they observe one they must report it or they are in fact part of the problem itself.

This is very tough medicine. Our advice, if confronted with this kind of behavior, is to

- React aggressively to any form of humiliating behavior. The perpetrator must know immediately that they have crossed the line.
- In less extreme circumstance, report it to your boss immediately and if it is your boss who is the culprit, then report it to the CEO. Put it in writing!

- If there is any form of assault or other illegality, such as a hate crime, then report it to the authorities as soon as you can.

The people who behave this badly are cowards and they are taking advantage of others who are in a subordinate position. No man or woman wants to be treated like this and no leader, male or female, should accept this behavior from anyone else.

What about employees who come to work dressed as if they are off to the beach? What about the company Christmas party where alcohol is freely consumed and inhibitions let down? What about office romances gone wrong? It sure is tough to be a leader in today's organizations.

What is clear is that a zero tolerance policy on any form of harassment is the only way for a company to continue engaging in business and protect the welfare of all employees. This policy should include:

- Regular reinforcement of a clear easy to understand code of conduct is essential and not just once per year.
- Dress codes are there for a purpose and should be clearly stated, appropriate for everyone without bias, and they should be enforced. Offenders should be sent home to change.
- Company functions should monitor and control the availability of alcohol. Proper management supervision should be in place for all company functions.
- It should constantly be reinforced to employees, including management, that when it comes to fellow employees there is no difference between at work or outside work. The code of conduct applies to them and their interactions with fellow employees at all times.

For times when all of the above fails there should be a clear, easy-to-follow escalation procedure where incidents can be reported without intimidation and investigations can happen quickly so that action can be taken.

The vast majority of men and women want to do the right thing. The organization's leadership needs to put in place an environment where the best performance of all employees can be realized and where offenders are dealt with quickly to remove their toxic presence.

EVOLUTION IN OUR THINKING

"Richard, we still have a lot of work to do. Many men are still in the dark ages in different parts of the world. Yet, there are hopeful signs and we are much more evolved as a society. Let me give you a couple of examples of this.

"An investment banker recently said to me, 'Twenty years ago I was a complete jerk. My attitude about women was *give me a break, come on, chicks on the trading floor?* I didn't want to see change. I liked the way things were.'

"He then shared how he had changed once he had a female boss.

"He said, 'It was like a different world for me. What women leaders bring is a different perspective. I wasn't open to that before. Now I see that we lead so differently and our ideas bounce off each other so well and we work together so effectively.'

"And this evolution in our thinking is not only happening at the leadership level in companies. I'm seeing it at all cultural levels. I recall a hot summer day in Copenhagen a couple of years ago. I was walking downtown and there were three laborers working outdoors with their shirts off. I noticed a young woman in shorts and a tank top coming down the street toward them, pushing her bicycle.

"I thought to myself: 'Oh boy, here it comes. One of these guys is going to say something objectifying the young woman, but there was nothing. They kept working and she walked past and on her way. How amazing and how far we have come."

"Barbara, it's a lot different than it used to be. I think men deserve a pat on the back for how far they've come in their attitudes and behaviors, but not enough of them are on board and they haven't come far enough."

ARE WE STALLED OR ADVANCING?

There are both men and women who truly believe in this objective and who have made progress within their organizations. However, the majority of men running corporations today must, to judge by their actions, believe that their companies would not be better if they had promoted women into management roles and their boards over the past decade.

The role of the board member is to act in the best interests of the corporation. Study after study has shown that a more diverse management structure, including women in meaningful numbers at all levels, will observe superior performance. Often you'll hear from the chair that there are insufficient female candidates to be considered for the board. My response is, "How many did you look at? How many were presented to you? How many did you interview? When exactly did you start this process, when you knew you had a vacancy or well before a vacancy existed?"

Given that board membership is often limited by term, you can predict with a reasonable level of certainty what openings are going to occur. This gives you years to prepare. Unfortunately, studies show that for many companies new board members are chosen from among people the existing board members already know. Sometimes they are personal friends and often someone known to the CEO. Other times they can be customers of the corporation.

Today's managers are well versed in the language of gender equality. You'll never hear a manager speak out in meetings against gender equality. Often what happens in meetings on this topic is that everyone nods in agreement, some positive comments are exchanged, notes of these comments are made, and people are relieved and go on to other business.

"I can remember pushing this issue quite strenuously at times in my career, Barbara, only to be faced with a room full of mostly silent men.

"Some men would voice support for the issue and if there were any women in the room I would typically get their support, or I would support them and their comments. Mostly we got silence. I remember that on several occasions the response was, 'Okay … are you finished with that can so we get into some real business?'

"This, of course, is meant to deflate my passion for the issue as well as to let everyone in the room know where this stands in the priority list of the company. Remember, no one has said anything negative about advancing women into senior management. No one has said that it will result in anything other than superior corporate performance. Yet these fruitless meetings occur regularly when corporations are not convinced that adding women to all levels of senior management and their board will improve corporate performance."

There are four signs of progress that encourage us in the belief that the world is going in the right direction:

1. Over the past two decades, women more fully participate in all aspects of business. This includes their roles on boards as well as at the management table.
2. Women are acquiring the skills, education, and experience at a faster rate than men which bodes well for their future participation.
3. Initiatives like the "30% Club" in the UK and the Ontario Securities Commission's "Comply or Explain" regulations in Canada are keeping these opportunities front and center with corporations and other stakeholders.
4. Men's attitudes are changing and they are prepared to go on record and voice their support.

So how do we respond to those who say progress is too slow or, in some cases, even seems to be slowing down? This too is true. However, the forces of change now being directed at the issue of women in business are truly formidable. We now have an educated workforce of women who are tired of hearing they are unqualified by those who run today's companies.

There are customers who want the companies they buy from to represent them and not some outmoded structure from the past. There are governments and regulators feeling burned by the last financial crisis that are ready to act if they see another market failure for which society will have to pay the tab. There are investors looking at the research and trying to figure out how they can model female engagement in predicting a company's future performance. Many tell us that they have never seen the potential for women to advance in business to be so close and so strong.

THE "AHA" MOMENT

"Lars Terney, a partner at Nordic Capital, is a leader who comes to mind, Richard. Lars started his career at Boston Consulting Group in Chicago in 1994, was one of the founders of BCG's Copenhagen branch in 1998, and became managing partner for BCG's Copenhagen office in 2001 and senior partner in BCG in 2007.

"Here's how he came to his 'aha' moment earlier in his career."

Some 15 years ago as a testosterone-filled, "know-it-all" early 30's male and newly appointed Managing Partner of BCG's CPH office, I was sitting listening to a young female consultant give a presentation of her analysis in the large conference room.

She was a bit exhausted having worked all night to get to analytical perfection and clearly very smart, but lacked assertiveness, seemed slightly insecure, somewhat down played her many, many analyses, scanned the room a lot for affirmations and reactions—and she didn't fully dare to conclude on her own. Do you believe your own analysis? Get to the point more quickly, I thought. Remembering how I myself would draw a line showing causality with just one data point.

But I had just attended some training on the general tendencies of differences in male and female behavior, and I pushed myself to "pause"—and not look at the style and behavior, but listen for the content. Not that this had any impact, but today, this young consultant is now the Managing Partner in BCG's CPH office.

I realized that the above story was likely my "aha moment." I am completely convinced that the neuroscience that underlies our gender differences is the key to further our thinking about Gender Diversity and the economic value derived. More generally, understanding our differences, which are strengths actually, improves our ability to work with differences in approach, style, focus, and opinions and is the key to better decision-making.[6]

There is no question that progress in advancing women into leadership, if measured over the long term, has been remarkable. There is also no question that some measures of progress have slowed or stalled, particularly in developed countries. However, there are significant grounds for optimism:

- Groups of women and men are forming in every country and these groups are pushing for more voluntary progress towards gender diversity in leadership.
- Governments are watching closely and have shown they will act if the public believes there is another market failure taking place.

- Regulators are prepared to act to force gender diversity transparency that has been missing from public company disclosures.
- Investors are starting to put their money into companies that meet certain tests for gender diversity in leadership.
- Many companies are implementing aggressive business sourcing and development programs targeted at women.

"To add to your last bullet, Richard, companies are expecting greater gender diversity from their suppliers and partners and tend to favor vendors that truly are diverse and not just saying they are or intend to be. It's like in the story I shared in Chapter 2 about the consulting firm who lost the project because of their poor record in advancing women."

BREAKING THE MOLD

"Barbara, we've mentioned several times in our book thus far that roughly 20 percent of male leaders 'get it' and are actively involved in the advancement of women in their organizations. Don Lindsay, president and CEO of Teck Resources Ltd., works in an industry that is quite different from that of financial services, yet shares the same challenges in recruiting, retaining, and advancing women into senior management. But Don has taken a profound step that has broken through conventional thinking and is successfully changing mindsets.

> Mining is often viewed as a traditional industry—and that's true, in many ways. For example, the career path for mine managers has been roughly the same for decades: engineers become superintendents; superintendents become mine managers; and mine managers become general managers.
>
> In addition, many mining jobs—such as haul truck driver, engineer, and mechanic—have traditionally been male-dominated. Unfortunately, these traditions have become barriers. Skilled, smart people who aren't on the "right" career path assume certain jobs are forever out of reach. Roles aren't always filled by the best candidate or go unfilled because female candidates feel discouraged from applying. And companies suffer as a result.
>
> I wanted to find a way to break the mold and send a strong message that any job at Teck—whether truck driver, mine manager, or senior executive—is attainable for anyone as long as they have the ability and the commitment.
>
> That's why in 2013, I asked Marcia Smith, our Senior VP of Sustainability and External Affairs, to take a leave from her current corporate role and become General Manager of our Line Creek mine for four months—the first female GM in Teck's 100-year history. While it surprised a lot of people at the time, it turned out to be a tremendous success.

I strongly believe taking that unprecedented step has helped create change within our company. It has inspired women to see themselves in different roles across Teck and encouraged managers to think differently about the type of people who might fill various roles. This has helped to break down barriers and, ultimately, make our company stronger.[7]

"In speaking with Marcia Smith, I discovered how, even in an industry that has been traditionally male since the first mine was mined, many men are accepting of women in leadership. Marcia had an interesting perspective on that."

It was incredibly daunting to be a general manager of a mine. Traditionally, general managers were men, and I was the first female in Teck's history of mining to be leading one of those operations. Nor did I have the traditional education and skill set that a general manager would typically have. That's been the pattern in the history of the company and in fact, most mining companies, but the person who took the job full time after me was a man without an engineering degree, so my presence broke down more than one barrier.

The most powerful stories for me were in the beginning, before I even started working at Line Creek. A woman manager in our finance group in Vancouver came up to me and said that a director position was available but she didn't initially apply for it because she didn't see women in senior positions and she didn't think she would get it. Then she saw the announcement about my becoming general manager of Line Creek and she applied for the director position and got it.

I hadn't even started working at the mine, yet the assignment was already having a positive impact in the organization. Women are looking for role models and seeing a woman in a leadership role gives others the belief that they can do it as well and succeed.

It's also important for men to see women in leadership roles. When I think back to the reaction of the male supervisors at Line Creek and even the frontline men while I was there: one third were enthusiastic and supportive and saw it as a sign of the future; one third had gotten past the fact that I was a woman, accepted it, and moved on with getting business done; and one third had a hard time getting past it. It was heartening to know that two thirds of the men were great with it and with moving our organization forward.[8]

"Marcia's estimation of the percent of men in support of women in leadership is very close to ours. What shattered the glass though at Teck was a male CEO who broke with tradition. Dean Windsor, the company's vice president of human resources, shared how the company itself has changed and is now looking at its talent in a whole new light."

Don Lindsay caught people by surprise by taking a woman out of the corporate office and putting her in charge of a steelmaking coal mine.

He did it purposefully to show that he was serious and to prove that competent women have the ability to take on any role within Teck.

Marcia was very successful in her time at Line Creek and I think it also changed the dynamic within that senior management team heading up our coal business unit. From a broader perspective, and through Don's leadership, we started looking at our talent review and succession planning processes and recognized that we needed to take some purposeful steps in promoting the development and careers of high potential, high performing women. We started giving these women leadership training, educational opportunities, and stretch-assignments on exciting projects. This is helping to raise women's profile in the company as well.[9]

We've shown evidence that promoting more women into management generates superior performance. We are in a world that sees clearly the improved corporate performance that happens when adding women to boards. Yet we are still moving in that direction much too slowly.

"Barbara, that reminds me of a famous quote by former Chinese premier Deng Xiaoping, someone I admire for his extreme perseverance. It's not the one that goes, 'to get rich is glorious,' although that lit a revolution in Chinese business. His other famous quote, which I studied at Peking University, was describing a journey as 'crossing the river by feeling for stones.'[10]

"Journeys filled with unknowns require us to proceed cautiously. Perhaps this is what's happening with women in senior management. We may be making progress but that progress is slow, as the risk of each step requires caution. Perhaps it is too slow for some, but it's also moving too fast for some others. The journey is proceeding even if some are afraid what the next step will bring."

Many men have already seen a need to change. This has led to the solid endorsement of the UK's "30% Club" by men. The organization has had significant support from women and men and is now going global. It is leading the introduction of new regulation in the province of Ontario for public companies to comply or disclose why their boards are less than 30 percent female. Many influential businessmen in the United States have aligned themselves with gender diversity in senior management.

We are at the threshold of dramatic progress in the evolution of companies. Investors are starting to take notice of those who most effectively utilize all of their human resources. Similarly, regulators and government are finding the pace of change slow and are discussing a number of new techniques to accelerate change. These heavy-handed approaches should not be necessary.

Market forces should provide the solution, which is to hire more women at all levels and advance them into management—to achieve a balance between women and men and know that together they will lead your corporation to optimal success. These are the reasons men will find it in their interest to change.

Name one other way you can achieve such superior results at no incremental costs, simply by embracing the idea and practice of gender balancing your management teams and boards. You cannot find better value anywhere!

ENDNOTES

1. Laura Kane, "Billionaire Warren Buffett Says Women Will Save the U.S. Economy," *TheStar.com*, December 29, 2012, https://www.thestar.com/news/gta/2012/12/29/billionaire_warren_buffett_says_women_will_save_the_us_economy.html.

2. Gender Intelligence Group, "Gender Surveys, 2005–2015."

3. Everett M. Rogers, *Diffusion of Innovations* (New York: Free Press, 1995), 10.

4. Ibid., 20.

5. IMDb quotes: "Unforgiven," Malpaso Productions, 1992, http://www.imdb.com/title/tt0105695/quotes.

6. Lars Turney, Partner Nordic Capital, in discussion with the Barbara Annis, March 2016.

7. Don Lindsay, president and CEO, Teck Resources Ltd., in discussion with Richard Nesbitt, August 2016.

8. Marcia Smith, senior vice president, Sustainability and External Affairs, Teck Resources Ltd., in discussion with Richard Nesbitt, September 2016.

9. Dean Windsor, vice president, Human Resources, Teck Resources Ltd., in discussion with Richard Nesbitt, September 2016.

10. Satya J. Gabriel "Economic Liberalization in Post-Mao China: Crossing the River by Feeling for Stones," *China Essay Series*, October 1998, https://www.mtholyoke.edu/courses/sgabriel/economics/china-essays/7.html.

Chapter 6

MILLENNIALS: FACTS AND FICTIONS

There is a belief out there—call it a hope or even an expectation—that the men of the millennial generation coming into business and government will be more inclusive, collaborative, communicative, and even more emotionally intelligent than the "knuckle-dragging" baby boomer men who currently fill the roles of senior leadership.

They believe that millennial men and women are more understanding of each other than men and women of previous generations. Actually, the belief is that young men are less aggressive and more inclusive than previous generations of men.

They believe young men and women are both seeking the same type of work environment where they can be their true selves and blend together.

> "Richard, this couldn't be further from the truth. This is simply an enlightened denial that generational differences exist. Those placing all of their hopes in this new generation are enlightened because they're committed at some level to the ideal of gender equality; yet they refuse to acknowledge that there are real, hardwired differences between males and females.
>
> "They actually believe that baby boomers have these differences, but millennials don't. They think that social change has eliminated or greatly reduced gender differences, but it hasn't."

IT'S NOT A GENERATIONAL ISSUE

Our biological differences don't change in the span of a generation or two—or even in the forty or so generations it takes to make up a millennium. These differences have been with us for millions of years and will be with us for millions to come. We're deluding ourselves into thinking that the challenge in advancing women into leadership is a generational issue.

Millennial men are not really that materially different from boomers in their attitudes about women at work and women in leadership. We see the similarities at work every day in how men think and act, regardless of their age. And not just in work but in their personal lives. We see the same of millennial women, patterns of behavior witnessed all over the world as we as humans pass through our decades.

Yes, the millennial generation has its cultural distinctiveness, and we'll cover some of those differences in this chapter. Yet millennial men and women today between the ages of eighteen and thirty-four share many similarities with boomers or even the silent generation when they were that age. For example:

Raging Hormones

"There's a large consulting firm that does a lot of traveling for client engagements. A young consulting team in their late twenties, with roughly equal numbers of men and women, travels together for big client meetings, conferences, and trade shows. After dinner one night, one of the guys started texting a woman on the team to come to his room for more drinks. Texts went back and forth between them as he pushed on and she pushed back, and although nothing happened that evening, the incident wasn't over.

"He brushed it off as a failed attempt and basically forgot about it. She reported it, though, and it got so difficult for her afterwards that she couldn't continue working there. The challenge for females, of all ages, is that they ruminate about events and can't let go as easily as men can. So events such as the ones we're talking about here tend to have a greater effect on women.

"Men often say that they don't understand how women think, and they really don't. But it's amazing how they are all ears when you begin to tell them.

"The way women think just doesn't always compute for men. They admit that to me all the time. I know male leaders in engineering who are very right brain and analytical and tell us that they just don't get the emotional side. They're like all thumbs mentally.

"These guys are high IQ with analytical abilities that are off the charts. But their emotional side, their abilities to read people and situations and sense emotions are low on other equally important charts. They openly confess that they just can't connect though many want to and try to. Many of the male executives in technology that we coach understand their deficiencies and make every effort to connect, but sometimes it's like they're visiting from another planet. They work at it, but it's just not natural for them. And these are all millennial men."

There is no question that growing up in the 1990s was a largely different experience than that of growing up in the 70s or even the 50s. Every generation's attitudes and value systems are shaped by their era. The influence of parents, education, and culture creates common experiences and values that distinguish them from people who grow up in another time. We've identified four themes that we believe distinguish the millennial generation from any other.

The Most Educated

A large part of the reason young women have made so much progress professionally is due to their strong educational foundation. Millennials raised to believe by their parents that a college degree was essential to any successful career is one of the forces making them the most educated alive today. The following chart (Figure 6.1) shows the percentage of each generation's completion of at least a bachelor's degree by gender at ages 18–33.[1]

Millennial women, in particular, have continued along the same trajectory of the boomer women before them and now hold more degrees on average than their male counterparts. In the United States alone, 27 percent of women aged 18–33 have earned at least one bachelor's degree, compared to 21 percent of men the same age.[2] In Chapter 4 we shared data on women receiving more college degrees than men in countries across the globe.

There have been many programs designed to get more young girls interested in STEM studies and female graduates are now entering industries where they had previously been excluded, such as engineering and computer science. But as we shared in Chapter 4, computer science is one of the highest pursued college degrees yet women's graduation percentages are dropping like a stone. As you'll read later in this chapter, long-standing issues regarding representation of women in employment and leadership that were present in previous generations also plague millennials.

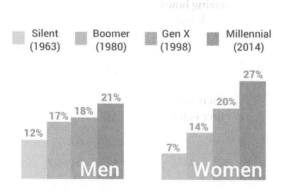

Figure 6.1 Millenials Are the Most Educated Generation to Date

Accustomed to Diversity

Most millennials never experienced life without a computer or smart phone, and the Internet was born around they same time they were. All this technology and the social media that floats on it has connected them to the diversity of the world in music, images, and concepts earlier in life and with more and a greater variety of information than at any time in history.

Cultural diversity programs are taught at all levels of education. There are over five hundred channels on television today compared to a handful when boomers were in their twenties. The fax machine and pager were considered high-tech tools in the 70s and the only mobile phones were of the variety that had to be installed in cars or about the size of a toaster oven.

Millennials are exposed to more gender and ethnic diversity in college and at the workplace than any generation prior. Many believe that millennial men's experience of seeing women in their college classes and working with them on their study teams and work teams will translate to millennial men being more accepting of women as peers and authority figures.[3]

> "Richard, it may be true that millennial men are more accustomed to *seeing* more women in education and on the job, but our data shows that millennial men are not necessarily on the same page when it comes to *understanding* the challenges female peers are facing when it comes to advancing in their careers."

And regardless of the greater presence of women by their side in universities and on the job, millennial men are no different from boomers in admitting to not understanding women.[4]

- 58% of millennial men say that both genders have an equal chance to advance
- 28% of millennial women believe that both genders have an equal chance
- 9% of men say they understand women
- 68% of women say they understand men

> "And just as with boomer men and women, millennials also desire to close that gap in understanding with 92 percent of millennial men *and* women saying that they could stand to improve their interpersonal communications with the other gender."[5]

Raised to Be Confident

Millennials were, by and large, raised to believe they could do and achieve anything they set their minds to. Many boomer parents, on the one hand, have been known to coddle their kids, fostering a sense of entitlement. Many parents, on the other hand, fostered a sense of possibility and growth, raising their sons and daughters to believe that they were equal to their peers and could be anything or anyone they wanted to be.

In their Own Words

Faye McDermid is a 33-year-old millennial who, with her family, emigrated from Iran sixteen years ago. These are her observations on what it's like to be a millennial woman working in engineering today, one of the most challenging fields for women, and how the self-confidence instilled in her by her parents has sustained Faye and enabled her to excel:

> When I first joined my company, I worked in their operations group, offering electricity to the marketplace. After rising to a supervisory level, I moved to electricity trading, which happened to be all men. I was actually the first woman to work in electricity trading, and a number of people warned me against going into trading, saying that it would be a rough environment for a woman. I knew it would be a career booster though, so I went for it.
>
> I've had to work harder than my male counterparts. In fact, if I had a choice between hiring myself or the men on my team, I would probable hire me, because I had to prove myself and my capabilities. Unfortunately, that hasn't meant that I succeeded more than men. There's still the male club out there.
>
> Millennial women that I know usually don't try out for roles until they think they're 100 percent ready. But I find that millennial men will promote themselves for positions with little to no experience, and learn along the way. I'm surprised how the men around me have asked for the promotion and gotten it with that mindset and I didn't and regret it. I could have been ready too once I started working at it.
>
> Millennial women I know who are my age can't imagine women not being able to fill any role today. They believe that if men and women are equally educated and experienced, they should be equally qualified.
>
> Millennial men I know are practical though when imagining whether or not a woman can fill any role. They acknowledge that there are some labor-intensive roles that women would have a difficult time contending with. But they mostly believe the higher positions such as a CEO, doctor, surgeon, judge, or prime minister can be filled by a woman or a man.

"Richard, Many boomer men in leadership share with me how they have been coaching their daughters since grade school to be more outspoken and feel more self-confident. And as their daughters have grown, many tell me that they mentor and advocate for their own daughters in their careers and that this is one of the reasons they are more committed than male leaders to seeing women advance to the higher ranks in their own companies."

This parental encouragement for so many young daughters, coupled with higher levels of education and connection through social media, has helped young women globally build self-confidence and pursue their own personal goals, whatever they may be.

Olivia and Lilly

"I reflect that attitude, Barbara, in how I did my part, alongside my wife, Lucy, in raising our daughters, Olivia and Lilly.

"At the onset, I wanted them to have every opportunity I had, and in a perfect world, to build on my success in banking. I certainly didn't want them to be held back because of their gender or to even think that restriction existed or held any water. I want them to be happy in whatever they decided to do and today I'm confident they will succeed because *they* are confident they'll succeed.

"Unfortunately, and maybe fortunately, banking is not their interest. My daughters don't want to give their lives to banking as I did. They've seen their dear old dad put in eighty-hour weeks driving a bank. I believe they want more out of life and they're already individually showing deep passion in their career interests.

"What's more important is that they have the self-confidence to pursue their dreams. I've always encouraged independent thought and an attitude that anyone can do anything they set their minds to do. I never imposed a distinction between what girls or boys could accomplish, or nowadays, what women or men their age can achieve.

"As a dad, I also made sure they attained their life skills—from learning how to fish to traveling on their own—pretty much paralleling my interests! We have a farm that we frequently spent time on over the girls' developmental years and I raised Olivia and Lilly to believe they could do anything a guy could do in that environment as well. I never set limitations in their minds.

"As they entered their teenage years, I taught them to be industrious and know what it's like to work for a paycheck. The girls have worked every summer since they entered the ninth grade. All of this Lucy and I hope helped to build on their being the independently minded, self-confident young women they are today and will be tomorrow."

Independently Minded

Through greater advantages for education and employment, millennial women have a greater sense of independence and are not feeling confined by family obligations as much as a generation or two ago. Their aspirations are to excel at work and at home. In fact, 66 percent of millennial women say they value career success, compared to only 56 percent of millennial men.[6] This parallels the numbers we in see in colleges and universities in North America and in countries across the globe.

Dr. Helen Fisher is the senior research fellow at the Kinsey Institute and member of the Center for Human Evolutionary Studies in the department of anthropology, Rutgers University. She is also the chief scientific advisor to the Internet dating site Match.com and has, over the past few years, compiled primary research on the attitudes and values of over thirty thousand Americans.

We asked Helen about the mindset that exists out there that we proposed at the beginning of this chapter, and her views about millennial men and women being different from that of men and women of previous generations. We were particularly interested in whether millennial men were different from that of boomers or the silent generation in attitudes and behaviors, and whether the generation of millennial men coming into business and government will be more inclusive, collaborative, communicative, and even more emotionally intelligent. Helen said:

> It's true that many of the differences that we are witnessing in millennials is due to the environment in which they've been raised. They live in a world very different from the environment in which their parents or grandparents were raised. Millennial women are better educated, self-confident, and more independently minded than their ancestors, a trend that actually began following World War I.
>
> We are in the middle of a social revolution, and that revolution is not technology driven but rather women driven, piling into education and the job market. Technology is certainly the enabler, but it's women's unshackled aspirations that are bringing about this revolution. Society is shedding hundreds of beliefs and practices of the agrarian tradition that have been around for 10,000 years, and moving forward to the kinds of male-female relations that men and women have always had and are meant to have.
>
> Even in the 1950s, the only way a young woman in her 20s or 30s could get to the top was to marry well. These days, women are putting off marriage until they've got their careers on track and they're financially independent. And more young women are buying homes before they marry than young men are. Today, they not only don't have to get married, they're choosing partners for different reasons based more on who they want versus who they need.
>
> As women's roles are expanding, men's roles are expanding as well. Many more millennial men than males of the preceding generations are willing to do household chores and look after the kids as their wife's career expands. The vast majority of millennial men in America want a wife who has a career. They don't want a stay-at-home mother.[7]

HOW MUCH THE SAME WE REALLY ARE

There are differences that this new generation brings, but to assume that millennial men will accept women into leadership with open arms and right all the wrongs either perpetrated or perpetuated by boomer men and the generations of good old boys before them is a false hope, and the technology sector is a perfect example of that fiction.

Silicon Valley is primarily millennial, and technology itself has a special attraction to millennials. They've been raised with tech gadgets since childhood, so they're comfortable in that environment. According to the U.S. Bureau of Labor and Statistics, the median age of employees in technology companies is about thirty-two. That's a full ten years younger than the median age of the entire U.S. labor force. [8]

The only career fields with median ages even close to what we're seeing in technology in the United States are bars (thirty-two), car washes (thirty), clothing stores (twenty-nine), restaurants (twenty-eight), and shoe stores (a twenty-four).[9]

Not only do technology companies have the youngest employees, but also the youngest men and women (primarily men) in leadership positions. Could this industry then be the first true test of millennial men's inclusive, collaborative, and emotionally intelligent attitudes and behaviors at the workplace?

We're not picking on the technology industry to prove our point, but given that this industry has the youngest age group and offers the most opportunity for careers for young people, we believe that regardless of this generation having its cultural uniqueness, the men and women of this generation are still males and females and share many similarities with the thousands of generations that have come before them.

Three of the largest companies in technology, Microsoft, Facebook, and Twitter, are each facing gender discrimination lawsuits, each filed in 2015. These are individual lawsuits at this point, though similar lawsuits filed against a number of pharmaceutical companies and banks over the past three years have more or less led to class action lawsuits and hundreds of millions in settlement charges.

A young female employee filed a lawsuit against Microsoft in September 2015 alleging that the technology giant discriminates against women in technical roles. The lawsuit states that female technical employees at Microsoft are paid less and promoted less frequently than men, and that their performances were ranked below than that of men.[10]

- At Microsoft, 72 percent of the employees, 83 percent of the technical workers and 83 percent of the leadership are men.

A former employee of Facebook filed a lawsuit in 2015 accusing the company of gender and racial discrimination as well as sexual harassment. She alleges that she was wrongfully terminated in October 2013 after she complained about being harassed and discriminated against by her boss and dozens of other male colleagues, based on her gender, race, and Taiwanese nationality.[11]

- Among Facebook employees, 84 percent of tech positions and 77 percent of senior leadership are men.

A former Twitter engineer has filed a gender discrimination lawsuit against her ex-employer, alleging that promotion opportunities are denied to women because of arbitrary promotion policies within Twitter that unlawfully favor men.[12]

- At Twitter, 90 percent of employees in technical roles are men; 79 percent of the management team is male.

In 2014, all three companies, with the best of intentions, said they were trying to bring more women into all levels of management and leadership. For years, technology companies have been silent about their diversity challenges—even to the extent of defending their silence by saying that the gender and ethnic makeup of their workforce was a trade secret. But behind the scenes, these same companies scrambled to find ways to increase diversity, offering some pretty fantastic perks, including high salaries, signing bonuses, day care, free cafeteria food, remote office days, and dry cleaning.

Google, where women make up 13 percent of the company's technical employees and 22 percent of its leadership, created workshops to encourage women to nominate themselves for promotions, offered longer maternity leaves, and made sure women interviewing at Google interviewed with women. Microsoft created "mentoring ring," a program designed to give its women employees more guidance from senior leaders.[13]

A *Harvard Business Review* study in 2008 featured fourteen innovative programs targeted at increasing the representation of women in science, engineering, and technology. According to the study though, just the reverse is happening. Because of hostile macho cultures, many science, engineering, and technology (SET) women arrive at the conclusion early in their careers that their success is dependent upon their ability to withstand aggressive male behavior.

The study went on to say that, as a coping strategy, women wanting to advance in their careers began to behave as men, adopting traditionally masculine attitudes and characteristics. In the study, one woman said she learned to shift from wearing skirts to wearing pants and using less makeup in order to increase her credibility at work. Fifty-three percent of SET women believe that behaving like a man improved their prospects for advancement.[14]

WHY WOMEN ARE NEEDED IN THE TECH INDUSTRY

As we noted in Chapter 4, in the early 1980s, young women earned 37 percent of computer science degrees and yet, in 2013, earned only 18 percent.[15] Its decline is sharper than in any other field of study.

When you consider the omnipresence of computers and smart phones in the lives of millennials and the universality of the Internet and social media, it stands to reason that computer science is one of the most popular majors in colleges. A career in technology offers great-paying jobs, a more stable career, and the ability to work with so many people of the same age.

The fact that women are not pursing college degrees in SET is also a problem for the tech-driven economy of the future. Computing jobs will more than double by 2020, to 1.4 million.[16] If women continue to leave the field, the shortage of qualified technologists will grow worse.

There's another reason women are needed in technology. Brenda Hoffman sees it as right- and left-brain thinking coming together to create superior products and services and a competitive advantage for companies with a better balance of men and women on product design and marketing teams.

Brenda Hoffman is senior vice president, head of global technology U.S. markets systems and global information services at Nasdaq. Brenda shares her experiences in working with millennial women and men who make up the vast majority of individuals on her teams. She speaks to each gender's inclinations and preferences in the field of technology and the critical need for the natural talents of women in technology to complement the natural talents of men.

> We have a strong program for internship here at Nasdaq and we draw 150 or so interns each year from top schools all over the country. The young men who come to us source from the traditional fields in technology, such as computer science and mathematics. Their interests are primarily in programming, development, and the electronic aspects of computing such as latency and bandwidth, or speed and capacity of the business applications.
>
> Many of the young women coming to us, however, are not from the traditional fields of study. Nor are they expressing career interests in programming, business requirements, or any of those functional roles. Even those who do receive their degrees in computer science don't want to be assigned to a specific task such as programming.
>
> Millennial women want the jobs that are on the visual side of computer programming. Some will show interest in the analytics behind the user interface, but they're generally more interested in how the mined intelligence will be presented back to the users. I see the genders splitting off that way.
>
> In a big way, computer programming parallels the two hemispheres of the brain: the analytical or left side of the brain, what I call the IQ of programming; and the visual, or emotional side, the EQ of programming. Men typically want to be on the IQ side while women generally express greater interest in EQ.
>
> It's interesting in meetings where women and men are working together on designing a system. The women prefer to visualize the design, put it up on the white board, and discuss it. They're more graphic and communicative than the men are. Men, on the other hand,

tend to visualize programming paths better than women and just want to start writing code—with less discussion. They're more comfortable working alone in a code-writing environment.

In capital markets, they're mostly coming to us with degrees in computer science, mathematics, and finance and are more interested in the information or intelligence that can be derived from the massive amounts of data that are continuously being generated from the vast number of sources.

Even the women who have computer science degrees are getting their masters degrees in distinctive fields of study. This will give women more opportunities for careers in technology, but companies have to recognize that the EQ of programming is as important as the IQ in defining the future of technology.

As organizations evolve their products and services to the visual age of technology, it is important for them to understand that women and men typically bring different though complementary skills. And it is the IQ and EQ, or left and right brain thinking, that are both needed for the future of technology. Women are naturaly strong in the EQ and men are strong in the IQ of how technology is created, developed, and deployed.[17]

IT'S NOT A GENERATIONAL ISSUE

The enlightened denial, which we spoke of at the onset of this chapter, of being committed to the ideal of gender equality yet refusing to acknowledge that there are real, hardwired differences between males and females, has kept us gender blind.

Denial had created and perpetuated our gender blind spots—the hugely erroneous assumptions we have about the other gender that persist in the absence of truth. Denial is causing miscommunication and misunderstandings about the beliefs and behaviors of the other gender. And this same enlightened denial has actually had its hand in preventing women from advancing in leadership.

It doesn't stop there. Our denial of hard-wired sex differences has placed a misguided hope on millennial men, believing that one generation of cultural influence can alter their brain physiology and magically make them more inclusive and collaborative than their fathers and grandfathers were, maybe even less aggressive and prone to risk taking.

There's no question that the world that millennials were born into and raised in has created some unique values and beliefs that were shaped by their world. Every generation does. But the advancement of women into leadership is not a generational issue, and hope and denial are going to let a lot of people down again.

We have to acknowledge that it's a gender issue. Moreover, it's a knowledge issue and, as mentioned earlier, many of the diversity training and development programs today offer very little in the way of knowledge building. In Chapter 7, we explain how and why.

ENDNOTES

1. Akane Otani "Proof That Millennial Women Are Taking Over the World," Bloomberg, March 20, 2015, http://www.bloomberg.com/news/articles/2015 -03-20/here-s-how-millennial-women-are-taking-over-the-world#media-1.
2. Ibid.
3. Darshan Goux, "Millenials in the Workplace," Center for Women in Business, Bentley University, November 2014, http://www.bentley.edu/centers/ center-for-women-and-business/millennials-workplace.
4. Gender Surveys, Gender Intelligence Group, 2005–2015.
5. Ibid.
6. Eileen Patten and Kim Parker, "A Gender Reversal on Career Aspirations," Pew Research Center: Social and Demographic Trends, April 19, 2012, http://www.pewsocialtrends.org/2012/04/19/a-gender-reversal-on-career- aspirations/.
7. Dr. Helen Fisher, Biological Anthropologist, Senior Research Fellow, The Kinsey Institute, in a discussion with John Fayad, senior associate, Gender Intelligence Group, July 7, 2016.
8. Steve Tobak, "Silicon Valley's Worst-Kept Secret: Ageism," Fox Business, May 4, 2015, http://www.foxbusiness.com/features/2015/05/04/silicon-valleys -worst-kept-secret-ageism.html.
9. Ibid.
10. Jessica Guynn, "Microsoft Sued for Gender Discrimination," USA Today, September 16, 2015, http://www.usatoday.com/story/tech/2015/09/16/micro soft-lawsuit-gender-discrimination/32505143/.
11. Tom Huddleston, "Facebook Is Sued for Sex Discrimination, Harassment," Fortune, March 18, 2015, http://fortune.com/2015/03/18/facebook-sex- discrimination/.
12. Natasha Lomas, "Twitter Latest to Face Sex Discrimination Lawsuit," TechCrunch, March 22, 2015, http://techcrunch.com/2015/03/22/twitter- gender-discrimination-lawsuit/.
13. Kia Kokalitcheva, "Google's Workplace Diversity Still Has a Long Way to Go," Fortune, June 1, 2015, http://fortune.com/2015/06/01/google-diversity- demographics/.
14. Ibid.
15. National Center for Education Statistics, "Degrees in Computer and Information Sciences Conferred by Degree-Granting Institutions, by Level of Degree and Sex of Student: 1970–71 through 2010–11," https://nces.ed .gov/programs/digest/d12/tables/dt12_349.asp.
16. Tracey Lien, "Why Are Women Leaving the Tech Industry in Droves?" Los Angeles Times, February 22, 2015, http://www.latimes.com/business/la-fi- women-tech-20150222-story.html.
17. Brenda Hoffman, senior vice president, head of global technology U.S. Markets Systems and Global Information Services, Nasdaq, in a discussion with Richard Nesbitt, August 2016.

Chapter 7

WHAT WORKS AND WHAT DOESN'T

We've shared a lot with you thus far, all of which we know and believe to be true—that if you want to realize improved financial performance, significant and sustained performance—you must hire and promote women alongside men into management, and elect them to your board of directors.

We demonstrated the business case for women in leadership and the ascent of women in education and commerce, across the globe. We acknowledged the rise of men in their advocacy for women leaders and shared stories of male leaders personally involved in making that happen. And we touched on the advances in neuroscience, deepening our understanding of gender differences, exposing our unique strengths and the value in the complement in the often distinct ways that men and women think.

"Richard, we're in the midst of a cultural transformation in organizations and in the world itself. It is not just about gender balanced teams and organizations, but gender-intelligent teams and organizations. It's knowledge that accelerates a cultural transformation. It's about men and women getting it and seeing the competitive advantage of gender differences and the impact that can have on the financial performance of an organization or the growth of a nation.

"When men really get this and stand side by side with women and walk the talk, it has a positive impact on the culture."

"Barbara, men often tell us that they don't know what to do. The chart in Chapter 5 on the three types of male leaders in their attitudes toward advancing women in leadership shows that 60 percent are believers. They recognize the value of women in leadership but don't know what to do or even realize that they need to be involved in the first place."

"Richard, the reason this chapter is here is because not just men, but organizations also, often don't know what to do or are doing the wrong things with the best of intentions. There are things companies have to do prescriptively to create that culture, but not by trying to fix women.

"Number one is that you have to get a critical mass of men to become aware of and understand the economic value of women in leadership, and in doing so, begin to recognize their own blind spots when it comes to advancing women."

"How to be a gender intelligent leader will be the most sought after leadership competency over the next twenty years; and leadership is what transforms cultures. So if you men out there want to be leaders in the future, then how to be gender-intelligent leader is what you need to glean from this chapter."

"Richard, that reminds me of an event that took place just last week. I witnessed, as I've been witnessing for years, the best of intentions of a man on the path to becoming gender-intelligent leader, in this instance, a CEO, very desirous of being on that path, but falling short of his goal. This is what I mean by recognizing one's own blind spots."

"If I Hear Another Father-Daughter Story ... "

The CEO of a large financial services firm was on stage, kicking off his company's corporate conference. He began to introduce me; I was sitting at the head table near the stage ready to stand and walk up. He took a few moments first to share his own awakenings about Gender Intelligence and was using his daughters as examples to show his progress and new insights. Also sitting at my table were a few of the high-level women executives in the company.

One of the women looked at the woman next to her and said, "If I hear another father-daughter story, I think I'm going to puke! Why does he always talk about his relationship with his daughters and not about his relationship with us?"

Another added, "I know. Haven't WE given him any gender-intelligent insights?"

The CEO's intention was to speak to his growth in Gender Intelligence, yet the way it landed on the women at my table, and I expect at other tables, was much different. This was a gender *un*-intelligent moment for the CEO.

He had great women colleagues all around him about whom he could have shared stories, but he had a huge blind spot that created incongruence between his intention and his behavior. Many male leaders are often so affected by their newfound knowledge of the science of gender differences that they apply it to their personal lives as well as their work lives. Thus, men often use examples of their Gender Intelligence in their relationships with their daughters. It could be the emotional attachment and deeper meaning for some, or not knowing how to articulate their intelligence work with their women colleagues. Whatever the reason, men have to become more actively conscious.

I'm not throwing the baby out with the bath water. Men are in ascent, which is what this book is all about and what we want to support. But this illustrates how gender-intelligent leadership needs to be a constant practice.

WE'RE OVER THE TIPPING POINT

Just as we shared in Chapter 5, the "tipping point" for a movement to catch fire is when the critical mass of early adopters reaches 13.5 percent.[1] In our estimation, 20 percent of men are gender aware and are acting on it. So we're beyond the tipping point for a movement. There's a difference here, though. The 20 percent of men in this instance are dispersed within companies across the globe, making it difficult to create a social movement that can "catch fire" and spread.

Yet, there is a way to accelerate culture change and that is through reviewing what works and what doesn't work across some of the more prevalent gender diversity initiatives and sharing that with the 60 percent of men who are believers of the value of women in leadership and want to know what to do. We want to shift 10 percent of that group to the small but active group of men who get it *and* are acting on it.

Caring and Hoping Isn't Going to Cut It

"Barbara, there are many reasons why leaders and their organizations fail to see the weaknesses in their gender diversity initiatives. You and I both spoke to those in Chapter 1 and we shared the epiphanies or "wake-up calls" that each of us had early in our own careers. The question remains though: Why do companies consistently trot out the same programs every year that consistently fail to achieve their objectives?

"My 'Brushing Horses' metaphor hinted that it might be that the corporation feels better for having taken action—for having done something. For some of these programs, the goal is really the appearance of caring about increasing diversity and hoping that something sticks.

"Senior management would never continue to expend resources on a program in any other aspect of their operation if it didn't deliver the promised results. They would modify their approach until they got it right or drop the initiative altogether and redirect the resources to something with a more guaranteed return. Increasing diversity and the advancement of women in management seems to be an area where some companies have accepted failure but then keep on doing the same thing over again each year, hoping for different results. Isn't that Einstein's definition of insanity?"

"Richard, I call it 'window dressing'—the appearance of the pursuit of equality. All too many companies establish gender initiatives to look good or to reduce complaints from employees and other constituencies that they're not doing anything. Diversity programs that are little more than a pretext of effort are destined to fail because they're not linked to the financial goals of the company and lack the full support of top leadership.

"The outcome is almost always the same—gender diversity initiatives may expand the number of women in the organization at the entry and middle management levels, but not so much at the top. There, the glass ceiling remains, which becomes indicative of a deeper and remaining challenge—the company's culture is not changing."

HOW TO CREATE SUSTAINABLE CHANGE

U.S. companies alone spend $8 billion a year on diversity initiatives with lackluster results. Why lackluster? If the ultimate intent is to increase the percentage of women in leadership, then the numbers, moving at glacial speed, tend to speak for themselves.

The Gender Intelligence Group recently conducted a detailed study to assess the diversity programs that create a sustainable impact in advancing women into senior management. We gathered data from three technology companies, four financial services firms, and two accounting firms to determine what works and what does not work.[2]

We first set out to understand the reasons the nine companies were focusing on gender. Why was it on their radar? In their order of importance, leaders in human resources, diversity and inclusion, and various heads in business units responded with this list of motivations. See how many of these ring true in your organization:

- A business imperative
- Problems recruiting women
- Problems advancing and retaining women at the senior level
- Higher turnover of women compared to men in mid-management
- Women at all levels scoring employee surveys lower than men at all levels
- Fierce competition for women's talent

We then asked company leaders to define the organizational barriers they came up against in their attempts to advance women into positions of leadership:

- A male-dominated leadership culture
- Lack of understanding of the economic benefit of gender diversity
- Bias toward male characteristics in recruitment and traits of merit-worthy leadership
- Absence of role models for women leaders and for male leaders to witness women performing and succeeding in leadership positions
- Outmoded preconceptions and traditional mindsets about the strengths of women and their role in business
- A lack of mentoring and sponsorship of high-potential women
- Work-life flexibility programs that didn't address the needs of women in senior leadership

When the leaders from the nine companies were asked what efforts they had taken to eliminate the barriers, the following eight programs were the most often mentioned. Four are presented here as those that are working well and moving that needle forward; and four others that have consistently failed to sustain any positive results and should either be modified to be successful or eliminated to free up resources.

WHAT WORKS AND WHY

Of the diversity programs employed by the nine companies in our study, these are the top four that leaders in our surveys claim had the greatest effect in creating a sustainable impact in advancing women into senior management.

Leadership Accountability

As a practice, leadership accountability effected the most positive change in the advancement of women into leadership positions across the nine companies that participated in the study. Leaders were held accountable for inclusive leadership competencies and behaviors using a 360 leadership tool. Company leaders reported quarterly metrics by gender for their departments and divisions such as employee engagement, advancement, retention, and talent management.

Yes, leaders have been held accountable before and on a variety of metrics. The problem is their half-hearted accountability. Male leaders, feeling forced to comply and not making the connection of balanced leadership to superior performance, often charge HR or D&I with the task of, say, increasing the representation of women in senior levels to 30 percent in two years.

Thinking that numbers alone will create a cultural transformation is no different than putting the cart in front of the horse. The only way to transform culture is by putting the horse out front. And the only way to get male leadership out in front and leading the transformation is to have them personally committed.

What made the practice of leadership accountability the *most* successful across these companies was that male leaders weren't motivated by compliance but rather by a deep personal commitment that came from their greater understanding of the economic value of gender diversity in leadership.

To build that understanding, a business case was developed for each company, customized to their particular industry. This dollars-and-cents argument was used as the rational for gender diversity, and in doing so, captured the attention of senior leadership, by presenting the case for women in leadership as a financial benefit even the most ardent cynic could buy into the logic.

The business proposition, combined with the neuroscience of gender differences, were the "motivational tipping points" encouraging leaders to move beyond opinions, suspend assumptions, and open themselves to new insights. The leaders in these companies began to view the advancement of women as a strategic imperative and directly linked to superior corporate performance. They then welcomed the accountability with open arms and got involved in attaining the numbers.

Gender Coaching and Training

As we shared in Chapter 2, knowledge building is often overlooked in the execution of personal development initiatives. Gender coaching and training programs were modified to become information sharing and awareness workshops and one-on-one coaching sessions intended to increase leaders' Gender Intelligence and knowledge of gender differences.

> "Richard, the first few moments of a Gender Intelligence workshop are fascinating to watch. The male leaders in attendance typically enter the room with their guard noticeably up. You could tell they've been through diversity training before. They expect to hear about quotas and what their number is going to be for their department or division for the current year. They often feel they're the ones to blame for women not advancing. So, in those first few minutes, the men are preparing to shut down. There's going to be no reason given for the new numbers aside from compliance and the pressure of it being the fair-minded thing to do. No knowledge shared, just blame, strategy, and implementation.
>
> "In these nine companies, knowledge building preceded strategy and implementation; and there was no blame placed on men. Once male leaders were presented with the business case for gender diversity and the neuroscience that underlies gender differences in critical thinking skills, they become strong advocates for the women in their organizations who are looking to advance.
>
> "It's like cataracts fall from their eyes over the course of workshop. They lean forward in their chairs and become sponges, absorbing the content and asking questions. Many declare their new knowledge during the session and their promise to be more actively conscious of their own behavior. The knowledge gained during gender-intelligent coaching and training provides the rationale for the strategy and implementation."

Male Sponsorship

Sponsorship programs that worked were modified to involve senior male leaders sponsoring high-potential women. As a result of gender coaching and training, male leaders were eager to sponsor the high potentials in their departments and cross-divisionally in a majority of companies in the study. Sponsorship training in one-on-one coaching sessions helped to develop in male leaders a solid understanding of their role as sponsors:

- To expand their view of the traits of leadership and open themselves to diversity in leadership and results driving techniques
- To be aware of the female talent in the pipeline who are up-and-coming and track their performance

- To mentor, empower, and encourage potential women sponsees
- To advocate for the sponsee at high levels of the organization
- If a direct report, to give the sponsee stretch assignments that will increase her visibility and advance her career

Other distinguishing factors found in the sponsorship programs included having women participating in the program to sponsees undergo a 360 assessment of their leadership competencies; show they have met or exceeded performance objectives over a two-year time frame; and to have charted out a five-year career plan. Another factor that contributed to the program's success was that many women sponsees had multiple sponsors from different divisions within their companies.

"Richard, many companies have mentoring programs but few have sponsorship programs. And there are a few who have a difficult time distinguishing between the two. Mentoring is long term coaching; sponsoring is personally advocating for an individual—putting your name on the line for that person.

"In successful sponsorship programs, male sponsors first act as mentors to their female sponsees, guiding them in the development of their five-year plan and helping them navigate the male modeled business environment and corporate ladder and negotiate the male code along each rung. That inside knowledge that can only come from a male sponsor is invaluable information to a woman being mentored and sponsored."

Succession Planning

Succession candidates became more diverse once the blind spot of assessing high potentials on the basis of sameness was removed. Well-intended business leaders often build meritocracies where the talented in the organization—regardless of their gender—are promoted based on their abilities and achievements. Their blind spot is in not seeing the built-in inequalities in their organizations when measuring performance. So when organizations say they are fair in promoting, they are actually looking for a very specific set of behaviors that tend to favor men during succession planning.

The modification in thinking created a gender-mixed and highly diverse slate of candidates. This improved line of sight into succession planning had senior leaders involved in removing similar blind spots in merit-based evaluations, candidate selection, and candidate leadership training and development.

Whether in decision making, managing projects, closing deals, or leading teams, women will often get to the same results, and oftentimes improve the outcomes, using a different path than men. Yet, in most meritocracies, sameness thinking is valued and rewarded over difference thinking.

For instance, in high-tech companies, software engineers and developers who are most valued and climb the ranks are those who are deeply analytical and extremely fast in the way they communicate. Similarly, in the financial services industry, aggressive and hard-charging behavior is highly rewarded. Many women with equal intelligence and a remarkable ability to think through complex problems and make well-informed decisions will often hold back in environments like these—and not be viewed as high potentials because of it.

As a result, many capable women have difficulty climbing the organizational ladder. And the few women that do manage to fit in and survive simply adopt and reinforce the existing male model.

> "Imagine, Barbara, if everything was reversed and women had developed the prevailing business model and the female code was something men had to work with and navigate every day. And imagine men being selected for succession based on the metrics of how well they did that. I wonder how long men would put up with it!"
>
> "Richard, the men would feel forced to play a part often the opposite of how they would naturally prefer to think and act. Men would feel as if they were working with their hands tied behind their backs. They would feel undervalued for showing behavior that didn't measure up to the standards set by the female-designed organization."

Some might argue that the business world is highly competitive, but the world is changing and expectations of leaders to be more inclusive, create engaged workforces, and seek win-win solutions to complex problems are growing.

In order for a meritocracy to work effectively, the metrics must be based on how men *and* women uniquely think and act. Differences need to be valued in order for meritocracies to be truly performance based and reflected in evaluations, promotions, and succession planning. And that's why succession planning is working across these nine companies.

Through the coaching and training initiatives just outlined, company leaders grew to realize that their meritocracies, based on gender sameness, were contributing to women's falling short in their advancement. Leaders modified and expanded their new talent management initiatives to recognize competencies based on the unique ways in which men and women approach business situations, make business decisions, and lead and manage teams.

The added benefit of applying a gender-intelligent lens to their sponsorship, new talent management, and succession planning programs was a significant increase in the recruitment and retention of talented women across the nine companies. They're achieving their quotas by putting the horse out in front of the cart.

WHAT DOESN'T WORK AND WHY

From our study of the diversity programs implemented by the nine companies in our study, these are the perennial programs that have shown minimal success. As we termed in Chapter 1, these are the diversity money pit programs that most often do not produce the desired results and why they are failing.

Diversity and Compliance Training

Survey results and one-on-one interviews with the male executives across the nine companies indicated to us that the "get your mind right" diversity and compliance training programs for men created a reverse effect. Men were trained to ignore gender differences and treat everyone the same, but they tended to become overly sensitive, politically correct and guarded in their language, and afraid to acknowledge any gender differences.

Here again, strategy and implementation are the focus of most diversity training efforts, rather than building knowledge first. The statistics we provided in Chapter 4 on the steady rise in sexual discrimination lawsuits since the 1990s, around the time when unconscious bias training was first introduced, suggest that diversity and compliance training hasn't delivered the desired results in self-awareness and behavior change.

There is little evidence that sexual harassment policies and training programs are effective at actually reducing harassment. In one study, researchers found that attending sexual harassment training did not have an effect on participants' knowledge about sexual harassment and, more important, did not make them less likely to engage in harassing behaviors.[3] In another study, participants who received sexual harassment training walked away from the training more confused about what constituted sexual harassment than before they walked in.[4]

A 2006 Harvard/Yale study looking at data from 708 private companies found that diversity trainings didn't produce more diverse workforces.[5] And a 2009 review by researchers from the University of California, Harvard, and the University of Minnesota of hundreds of studies showed that the effects of most diversity efforts, including training, remain unknown.[6]

Companies are leaping on unconscious bias training without making sure it's being deployed correctly. A 2014 study showed that telling people everyone is biased "makes them more likely to act on those biases." One of the study's authors noted that people tend to imitate other people's behavior, and unconscious bias training suggests that it's normal for people to stereotype. Men walk away less motivated to change their behavior.[7]

There are more negative effects from sexual harassment training and unconscious bias training that are not being revealed in these studies, but male executives often confide those "terrors" to us. Many have the fear of unconsciously saying or doing something wrong or insensitive. They tell us that they've become cautious and brief in their discussions with women; many have difficulty giving critical feedback to women on their teams; and some even admit that they avoid interactions with women, especially in informal settings.

Training for Women

Coming up a close second in unsuccessful training initiatives is training for women, which often tends to place the onus on "fixing" women. Many of the companies' management and leadership development programs, as mentioned earlier, were initially designed for their male leaders and were now being used to define women's leadership and essentially help them fit into a sameness model—instead of mining for their own unique leadership styles.

Creating "Bully Broads"

Silicon Valley has always been the mecca for skilled technologists coming out of college. It was that way for young women with science, engineering, and technology degrees during the 1990s and early 2000s. Many became skillful women leaders and worked hard against many odds to advance in their careers. We've defined those challenges in Chapters 4 and 6.

In order to lead teams made up primarily of men and to negotiate with vendors and partners, many women executives went through "assertiveness" training courses. The intent was to teach them to stand up for themselves and to express their own opinions, needs, and feelings without hurting the feelings of others. The goal was to teach women how to disagree without being offensive or aggressive.

Characteristically, the training programs offered to women were based on male models of behavior. Women executives were taught to solve problems sequentially and quickly and without emotion, make swift unilateral decisions, and be task-driven and goal-oriented.

Without an appropriate female gender model showing just how to be assertive, women became tough, forceful, and persistent, emulating the only models they had—men in leadership positions. Assertiveness became aggression and the term "bully broad" surfaced, describing the behavior of forceful, uncompromising women leaders who were brilliant, but failing in their careers.[8]

A program to "take the bully out of the broad," inclusive of 360-degree assessments by subordinates, peers, and supervisors, revealed that virtually every one of the women executives who participated in assertiveness training programs scored high on many of the negative traits commonly associated with aggressive behavior including abruptness, criticism, intimidation, irritability, and control.[9]

Men often state that they don't know how to report to women who act aggressively. They don't know how to work alongside them as colleagues or supervise them. Women trying to assert themselves but acting aggressively while doing so tends to confuse men and put them on guard. Their response is to minimize their interaction with or avoid those women altogether.

The solutions include the visibility of successful women in leadership positions as role models—for both women and men to see. Training programs for women should also be reviewed with a gender-intelligent lens to make sure that the program content develops women's strengths in critical thinking, empathy, and collaboration, and unique strengths in conflict resolution.

Women's Networks

Whatever they are called—women's networks, councils, or chapters—these initiatives often failed because they were not strategic and linked to the financial objectives of the company. They became little more than social networks. Meetings often became a venue for voicing complaints, but not linked to any initiatives in order to drive positive change. Some women admitted in confidence that the networks increased their sense of separateness from the rest of the organization.

"It's still happening today, Richard. Whenever women's councils or networks invite us in to give a keynote or seminar on how women can advance in their leadership and careers, we ask what percentage of the audience will be male. It's almost as if we're speaking a different language.

"It either doesn't dawn on these groups that male leaders and influencers need to be involved or that they would even be interested in women's career issues. Some confess that they really don't know how to go about getting men to participate."

"Barbara, one of the things that has become de rigueur in financial organizations is that CEOs need to have risk training and it's quite common for CEO candidates to be passed through the chief risk officer position. So let's parallel that. If building diversity and management in leadership are so important why wouldn't we want to ensure that future CEOs also take responsibility for diversity and hold the position of chief diversity officer for a brief stint as well?

"Just as they would become CRO for a period of years, they should also during their formative career become the chief diversity officer. They should be trained and tested in that position before they become CEO. I've never heard anyone recommending that aspect of succession planning. Have you?"

"No I haven't, Richard. I think it's a great idea. Given that this is so important to the future of the organization, it should be a required experience for any candidate seeking the position of CEO. Chief diversity officer will be more regarded as a senior management role, and strategic to the organization. In fact, it would bring more attention to that role."

Work-Life Flexibility Programs

Work-life flexibility programs are of great value to many women, especially at the entry and mid-management levels. They tend to work well as a recruitment strategy, but have little impact on advancing women to senior positions. Many of the senior women executives we speak with are not able to take advantage of the policies.

They're not as relevant to them any longer for family planning and parenthood as they might have been when they first joined with the company in their twenties or thirties.

Even in countries that legislate that companies must comply with work-life flexibility policies, women's representation in senior management is no better than the global average.

For example, 85 percent of the companies in the Nordic nations offer flexible working programs, yet women's representation in senior management is no different than the global average. And these Nordic countries have the longest history in gender diversity initiatives.

The same gap exists with the percent of companies offering flexible work-life programs in countries such as Germany (76%), the United Kingdom (67%), and the United States (62%). Yet, only one in five women are in senior management in these countries—percentages that have hardly changed in the past two decades."[10]

Male leaders and their companies are deluding themselves in thinking work-life flexibility programs are the solution and often blame women for not returning. The first step in making work-life flexibility programs work is to recognize that they are great for recruitment and meeting recruitment targets, but are often not helpful in the advancement of women.

OTHER BEST PRACTICES

The purpose of this chapter is to share with male leaders and their companies the types of diversity programs and initiatives that work and don't work in advancing women into leadership. We've watched some successful and not so successful programs emerge from grassroots efforts in companies and, through a gender-intelligent lens, we have supported and refined their efforts, bringing more men into the "get it and are acting on it" column, and resulting in more women moving into positions of leadership.

Role Models for Women and Men

"Barbara, I invite a guest speaker to address each session of the MBA program that I teach at the Rotman School of Management. And I've been very careful to ensure that those speakers are a blend of men and women. I think it's important for the women MBA candidates to hear from women leaders who are senior executives at companies or running their own businesses. But I think it's even more important for the men in my class to see women in positions of leadership in the financial industry and in other industries. It's important for men to see women in leadership roles."

"Richard, I couldn't agree more. Men need to see women in leadership roles with greater frequency. During our workshops, when attendees are asked to name some women leaders—in business or in government—men and women have a hard time thinking of more than one or two. The same problem exists within a company.

"We suggested to a client in the oil and gas industry, where there are very few women at the top, to publicize their women leaders in their corporate-wide newsletter, but not just the one or two in senior management, but those in succession planning. Job rotation is critical for advancement in this industry, as it is in many, but oil and gas is a little different. Rotation requires spending time in various posts where women are seldom ever found such as working offshore on an oil rig or out on a tanker in the North Sea.

"There are so many young women graduating with engineering degrees who want to work in the energy industry because they want 'to make a difference.' Seeing a story in the company newsletter and on the corporate website of a woman as the captain of a tanker is inspiring for young women at entry and mid-management levels. It not only aids in retention of young talented women engineers, but also can be used as a recruitment tool."

Gender Intelligent Sourcing and Recruitment

Speaking of recruitment, we also recommend that companies, particularly those in the more male-dominated industries, review their job descriptions, company profiles, and company social media for unconscious gender bias in word choice. A study conducted by the University of Waterloo at Toronto and Duke University shows that women job seekers were more interested in male-dominated jobs when advertisements were unbiased.

As an example, women and men may equally desire an engineering position, but highly masculine wording used in a job posting reduces the appeal for women because such language signals that women may not fit or belong. For this reason, qualified female, as well as male applicants, are opting out of jobs that they could have otherwise performed well in. The study also showed that male-themed words had the greatest effect on women, alerting them to the possibility that they will not fit or do not belong.[11]

Male-Themed Qualifications

"*Strong* communication and *influencing* skills. Ability to *perform individually* in a *competitive* environment. *Superior* ability to *satisfy* customers and manage company's association with them."

Female-Themed Qualifications

"*Proficient* oral and written communications skills. Collaborates well in a *team* environment. *Sensitive* to clients' needs, can *develop warm* client *relationships*."

The study, published in the *Journal of Personality and Social Psychology* didn't say why differences in wording had the greatest effect on women, but we believe it may very well have something to do with the female anterior cortex that we spoke of in Chapter 3 and women's on-average greater propensity to read the room better than men and to take in meta messages around facial expressions for deeper meaning. That ability is not limited to the visual sense, but includes women's inclination to seek deeper meaning from their entire environment. Men can often be of singular focus and will often scan the responsibilities in a job description and only zero in on the title and salary.

This turns out to be another finding in the study—that men were generally unaffected by the altered word choices used in the job and company descriptions.[12]

CRITICAL MASS AND CRITICAL MINDSET

We said earlier in this chapter that when it comes to advancing women, the number one effort is to get a critical mass of men to become aware of and understand the economic value of women in leadership, and in doing so, begin to recognize their own blind spots.

Paralleling that, we have to let go of the belief that men and women are the same. That mindset underlies most all diversity and compliance training today and is flawed thinking and must change. We need to implement the kind of training that stresses greater knowledge of the gender differences in how men and women complement each other so well in their often distinct thoughts and actions.

> "Richard, this is also about men building their own leadership practice. For instance, heart surgeons are continuously working at their practice, constantly learning and perfecting their technique. In a similar vein, great leaders are constantly building their practice, day by day, moment by moment—fine-tuning, perfecting, and learning more about their leadership style and ability to lead others. That truly is what leadership is all about.
>
> "In this context, leaders can have the best of intentions, which many men do have, but they can have incongruence between their intentions and their actions. We saw that earlier with the CEO talking about his daughters when he should be using his women leaders as examples and role models for others in the organization.
>
> "Men, work at building that congruence. We know you care. We know you want to see women succeed. You know the business case is there and it makes business sense to your company and to you personally. You can see the science and know the value of the authenticity that lies within men and women. Build your practice of leadership around this knowledge."

ENDNOTES

1. Everett M. Rogers, *Diffusion of Innovations* (New York: Free Press, 1995): 20.
2. Gender Intelligence Group study, "Best Practices in Gender Diversity," 2011.
3. Kim Elsesser, "The Real Problem with Diversity Programs: Too Many Lawyers," *Forbes*, January 5, 2016, http://www.forbes.com/sites/kimelsesser/2016/01/05/the-real-problem-with-diversity-programs-too-many-lawyers/#36a3d44075b0.
4. Ibid.

5. A. Kalev, F. Dobbin, E. Kelly, "Best Practices or Best Guesses? Assessing the Efficacy of Corporate Affirmative Action and Diversity Policies," *American Sociological Review* 71 (August 2006): 589–617, https://www.cfa.harvard.edu/cfawis/Dobbin_best_practices.pdf.

6. E. Levy Paluck, D. Green, "Prejudice Reduction: What Works? A Review and Assessment of Research and Practice," *Annual Review of Psychology*, 60 (August 2009): 339–367, http://static1.squarespace.com/static/5186d08fe4b065e39b45b91e/t/51e3234ce4b0c8784c9e4aae/1373840204345/Paluck_Green_AnnRev_2009.pdf

7. Elen Huet, "Rise of the Bias Busters: How Unconscious Bias Became Silicon Valley's Newest Target," *Forbes*, November 2, 2015, http://www.forbes.com/sites/ellenhuet/2015/11/02/rise-of-the-bias-busters-how-unconscious-bias-became-silicon-valleys-newest-target/#8d84417cb1f7.

8. Ibid.

9. Ibid.

10. April Mackenzie, Dominic King, "Women in Senior Management: Still Not Enough," *Grant Thornton International Business Report*, 2012, http://www.grantthornton.ae/content/files/ibr2012-women-in-senior-management-master.pdf.

11. Danielle Gaucher, Justin Friesen, Aaron C. Kay, "Evidence That Gendered Wording in Job Advertisements Exists and Sustains Gender Inequality," *Journal of Personality and Social Psychology*, American Psychological Association, March 7, 2011, https://www.hw.ac.uk/services/docs/gendered-wording-in-job-ads.pdf.

12. Ibid.

Chapter 8

THE ROLE OF THE BOARD

There is one aspect of business on which there can be no debate and no excuses. Boards of directors that are diverse create superior performance in their firms compared to those that do not have diverse boards. There is no reason why boards cannot be diverse given that boards themselves (and the shareholders) control who is on the board.

"Let me ask you a question, Richard. Is it fair to say that, in reality, most boards have very little influence on impacting the advancement of women in the companies they serve?"

"Barbara, your assumption is right to a certain degree. If the CEO doesn't want to do it, it generally isn't going to happen. The movement in an organization must begin with the board itself and they can act as a role model for the organization; and there is a correlation between putting women on boards, and, with a bit of a lag, the increasing presence of women in senior management. So something is happening there.

"There are also CEOs who tend not to follow the board but rather, lead the board in appointing women to leadership positions. And we have an example of one such man and his rationale a bit later on in this chapter.

"The role of the board member is to act in the best interests of the corporation. Study after study has shown that a more diverse management structure, including women in meaningful numbers at all levels, will result in superior performance.

"Often you'll hear from the chair that there are insufficient female candidates to be considered for the board. My response is, 'How many did you look at? How many were presented to you? How many did you interview? When exactly did you start this process? When you knew you had a vacancy or well before a vacancy existed?'

that creates the insufficiency of female candidates or new members being friends and acquaintances of existing members. There are other factors keeping the percentage of women on boards from growing."

LACK OF MENTORING

A recent survey conducted among 1,305 first-time directors along with 1,152 of their board colleagues at the 2,000 largest companies in the United States revealed how much mentoring first-time directors receive from incumbent corporate board members when they begin their directorships.[1]

Mentoring would include specific advice regarding the board's culture, protocols, etiquette, and any gaffes made by first-time board members. The survey showed that female and minority first-timers received this kind of mentoring far less often than their white male peers did. Racial minorities were 69 percent less likely to receive mentoring and women were 72 percent less likely.[2]

It potentially exposes how deep the currents run in an old boy's club. Not only did first-time women and minorities get significantly less mentoring than the men did, but such lack of guidance had a real impact. A shortage of advice reduced the chances that women or minority first-timers would be invited to join a second corporate board within the next two years by 57 percent.[3]

Less mentoring means making unforced errors, which can lead to fewer invitations for women and minorities, shorter tenures, and ultimately fewer appointments. And the great irony of all is that this "mini me" cycle of male directors selecting members in their own image is eliminating some of the most qualified directors. On average women and minorities in the study had significantly higher levels of management expertise, provided more advice and information to CEOs, and offered more highly rated knowledge and insights than did their male peers.[4]

STEREOTYPES IN BUSINESS

"Barbara, I now know that women and men are different. As a leader, I have actively sought this difference in bringing women into management teams with men because I believe that this diversity leads to better outcomes. However, what usually goes through a man's head when it is suggested more women are needed on the board is a picture of the last argument they had with their wife or the last scolding they got from their mother. There is no way these women could be on a board alongside them.

"Everything at a board meeting follows a defined set of rules: under these rules, men can discuss business. But if you let your wife on the board, she will bring up the time you ran into a post and were not looking where you were going. If you put your mother on the board, she will invariably bring up the failures of your youth and embarrass you as she did at the last holiday get-together.

"Of course, this is a ridiculous reason for not having women on boards—just as ridiculous as if men were all viewed as drunken, couch-sleeping, football-watching, insensitive braggarts who only pretend to be qualified for the job they are doing. Ouch, that gets too close for comfort! My point is that stereotypes have no place in business decision making."

RICHARD'S STORY: BOARDS IN THE 2008 FINANCIAL CRISIS AND THEIR GENDER COMPOSITION

"It's unfortunate, Barbara, that the management expertise and highly rated knowledge and insights that women and minorities bring weren't a counterintuitive force during the financial crisis of 2008.

"That fiscal and economic disaster was a defining moment in my life and career. It caused me to change jobs and take on challenges that I had never envisioned as part of my career path. One of the pieces of advice I give young people is: you can do all the career planning you want, but unexpected events will have the greatest impact on your career direction and your life. That does not mean you do not plan. You should plan incessantly. Planning is a way to be ready for these unexpected changes when they do happen. You prepare yourself with education, experience, savings, and family stability in order to pursue that unexpected offer when it comes your way.

"So anyway, there I was in 2007, happy as a clam, running a stock exchange that had seen little evidence of trouble in the general economy or the markets. Not only that, but in December 2007 we had just agreed to purchase the Montreal Exchange in the largest ever reorganization of market infrastructure in Canadian history. Within weeks of that event, I was chairman and CEO of the investment bank of Canadian Imperial Bank of Commerce (CIBC) and in a front-row seat to ride out the impact of the credit crisis.

"Let us get back to our hypothesis. That is, boards produce better results if they include both men and women. Would the boards of banks have been better able to withstand the impact of the credit crisis if their boards had been more diverse? We will never know. However, we can find some evidence that straight-line thinking may have contributed to the worst performances in the crisis.

"Research has shown that adding women to boards increases diversity of thought, increases the number of questions asked, and increases the amount of time boards spend on decisions in discussion. These are all qualities that would be seen to be in short supply at some banks during the credit crisis.

"'Too much sameness stifles critical thinking and breeds complacency and overconfidence, the combination of which can yield practices such as the kind of 'crony capitalism' that helped bring us the 2008 banking crisis,' said Rosabeth Moss Kanter, a Harvard Business School professor and one of the most influential longtime researchers in the area of leadership."[5]

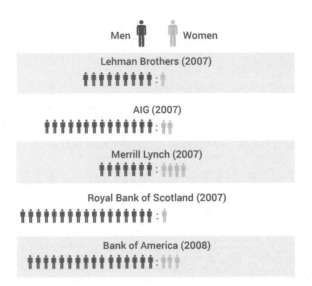

Figure 8.1   Boards of Directors' Gender Composition during the 2008 Credit Crisis

"Now, there's a statement that could whip up controversy. 'Crony capitalism' caused the credit crisis of 2008. Let me think about that statement for a minute (see Figure 8.1).

"Ms. Kanter, are you telling me that:

- "the nine men and one woman on the Lehman Brothers board of directors ...
- "and the sixteen men and three women on the Bank of America board of directors ...
- "and the fourteen men and two women on the AIG board of directors ...
- "... were engaged in what kind of capitalism?"

What Were the Seven Men and Four Women on the Merrill Lynch Board of Directors Doing?

"I have always thought that the shareholders of Merrill Lynch should have had a parade for Merrill's board and management for being shrewd enough to tie up with Bank of America before the bottom really fell out of the financial markets. Now let me see: four out of eleven equals 36 percent women directors at Merrill Lynch versus three out of nineteen, which equals 16 percent of women directors at Bank of America. A coincidence?

"Just for fun let's have a look at Royal Bank of Scotland. Oh great Scott! There are seventeen men and one woman on the RBS board of directors. I wonder how they fared?

"OK. I just can't help having a little fun. Of course, this was a long time ago in a galaxy far, far away. It was way back in 2008 and of course it was complex and of course I could still hear them say, 'Richard you really do not understand our business.'

"What happens when almost everyone in the group has a virtually identical outlook? Well, the following is a good explanation by Dr. Evan Apfelbaum, career development professor at the MIT Sloan School of Management."

> Homogeneity can lead individuals to underestimate the actual complexity of group tasks because they assume that others' behavior is more predictable than it actually is. People in homogenous groups tend to believe that because others look like them, they are like them in terms of having similar perspectives, knowledge and behavior. The assumption of like-mindedness feels comfortable; it caters to our basic human need for social acceptance and inclusion. But it also creates blind spots in our judgments and behavior. We underestimate the potential for seemingly similar others to have substantively different perspectives and ideas, which can lead us to make oversimplified, perhaps even, objectively inaccurate assessments in these contexts.[6]

THE QUOTA EXPERIENCE IN NORWAY

For years, companies have been talking about Norway and their experience with quotas for women's involvement on company boards. We found that all people really knew was that there have been quotas for women in senior management in Norway since 2006. Like a lot of other people in North America, we know almost nothing about Norway except that they ski and have wisely saved a lot of money from producing oil in the North Sea, unlike other countries.

It seems only fitting, given the topic we are discussing, that we should break away from our Anglo-Saxon obsession (the United States, UK, and Canada) and take a look at a slightly more exotic experience. Their story is fascinating, and it must have sparked more than a few emotional debates around dinner tables in Oslo, Trondheim, and farther afield.

In 2002, Norway had a three-party Christian-center-right government with the conservative Ansgar Gabrielsen as the minister of trade and industry. In the spring of that year, he sent the first shock waves through the Norwegian media by declaring that he was, "shit tired of the boys club because they did not take women on board." His patience with the "boys" was obviously coming to an end, and he warned them that if they did not pull themselves together, he would take actions most unlikely to come from his office and "would not refrain from proposing a quota law. People will be surprised to see the radical means I am willing to apply."[7]

In 2003, the Norwegian government decided that they would impose the need for public companies to have a minimum of 40 percent of their board of directors be female by 2008. The penalty for failing to comply with this law would be dissolution of the company. The number of public companies fell from 563 in 2003 to 179 in 2008. That meant that there were 570 female board positions left reserved for women out of a public company total of 1,400 in 2008. Private companies, on the other hand, had 90,481 directorships filled by women out of a total of 500,000 available.[8]

Norway's experience with quotas is fascinating. We can learn from the way they were introduced (by men), the reaction from public companies, and the massive number of delistings.

PICKING THE BEST CANDIDATE REMAINS VITAL TO SUCCESS

Women and men are obviously two different groups in society. Their unique identity begins from the moment of birth when they begin to build diverse experiences. Women and men may choose to acquire different tools through training, or they may acquire the same tools. Even though men dominate certain professions, in every profession there are successful women:

In *The Difference: How the Power of Diversity Creates Better Groups, Firms, Schools, and Societies*, Scott Page, social scientist and Leonid Hurwicz Collegiate Professor of Complex Systems, Political Science, and Economics at the University of Michigan, makes a good case for the beneficial effects of diversity—the difference perspective—for the functioning of social structures, at every scale.

> Teams of people with diverse training and experience typically perform better than more homogenous teams. Studies that isolate diversity in skills, such as between the types of engineers, show evidence that diversity improves performance. Studies of creativity and innovation conclude that cognitive variation is a key explanatory variable. Studies also show that management teams with greater training and experiential diversity typically introduce more innovations.[9]

Discrimination in society is often based on the perceptions and behaviors of the group to which you belong. We saw in Chapter 2 that a chairman felt that board members in Norway should have certain training, and this is what excluded women from the board candidate list. When the facts were examined, the male board directors did not all have the training their chair felt was essential. However, the chair's requirement was applied more rigidly to women candidates. This is the reason every leader must check the "plumbing." Check the systems by which you make choices relating to people. Check for bias in the selection of the requirements and check for bias in their application.

Dr. Page suggests that productivity emerges from creative organizations and environments with individuals from vastly different backgrounds and life experiences, bringing more and different ways of seeing a problem and, thus, faster/better ways of solving it.

> The belief that the best group consists of the best individual people rests on faulty logic. Instead the best collections contain people who are both diverse and capable.[10]
>
> That's why Google doesn't pursue a strategy of hiring only the people with the best grades from the best schools. In its own description of "who we're looking for," Google's first criterion is diversity. The company states that it is looking for diversity in training, experience, and identity with computer science graduates from Santa Clara working alongside former math professors. But Google is aware of the calculus condition (all problem solvers are smart). It seeks diverse people with knowledge of mathematics and computer science. It is not seeking poets.[11]

"Barbara, no one has ever said that we can just start picking employees at random and this will result in a better outcome for boards and management teams. But looking for diverse candidates that bring the ability to contribute will pay off more than sticking with the same criteria. When I sent my recruiting teams to university campuses, we were looking for 40 to 50 percent gender diversity. Given that graduate business programs are less than 35 percent gender diverse, it makes it very difficult to achieve this task. But cast your net wider. The graduates of the undergraduate business programs are 57 percent women. Why not hire these graduates and invest a little of the money saved in training?

"Furthermore, who says you need to stick with only business school graduates? Women are succeeding in a variety of professions outside business. Remember, your board is already overweight with businessmen. Why not look in government or politics or health care or the arts. There are many successful women in every field you could imagine. If they lack a specific skill then provide training, just like you would for a man.

"We learned in Chapter 6 that Brenda Hoffman, the CIO of NASDAQ, is taking this very approach in hiring women into the trading firm's IT organization. She sees the need for women in technology who can bring more left-brain into product design and marketing to complement men's right brain focus—what she terms the 'EQ and IQ of programming coming together.'[12]

IT MAY ALL START WITH THE BOARD OF DIRECTORS

We have seen throughout the research findings that the addition of women to boards of directors improves the performance of the firms. How does a board do that? Boards have lots of power but are limited in how they can exercise that power.

They pick the CEO, approve strategies presented by management, and approve corporate change such as mergers and acquisitions. They also approve capital budgets, compensation, and perfunctorily approve large contracts and regulatory submissions. We call all of this corporate governance.

Some critics of boards feel that much of this work is of little importance. Irving S. Olds, the chairman of U.S. Steel during the years 1940 to 1952, once opened a speech by proclaiming, "Directors are like the parsley on fish—decorative but useless."[13]

Some more recent observers admit to the importance of boards but not always to their effectiveness. John Schnatter, chair of Papa John's International Inc. observes, "Behind every Freddie Mac, Bear Stearns or Lehman Brothers who led their company down the path toward financial ruin, there was a board of directors that sat by silently and let it happen."[14]

We do not agree with these critics. Boards are important to the ongoing success or failure of a company. There is no substitute in today's modern economy for boards being given ultimate and overall responsibility for the governance of companies. However, that should not stop us from trying to improve the performance of the board. Let's stay on this theme.

Boards can be a major source of what we term "gender success," which, as we discussed earlier in *Results at the Top*, is the strategy of employing gender diversity in the leadership of your company in order to produce better results.

Let's Walk through How They Do That

A. **Boards choose their own gender composition**

Board's themselves decide on the makeup of its members. Of course, the slate of directors that the board proposes must be approved by a majority of shareholders. In our experience, the slate recommended by the board is rarely not approved. In the case of gender choice of director candidates, this has always been the choice of the board itself. In today's configuration, the boards themselves have decided that the right composition should include mostly men.

B. **Boards choose the gender of the CEO**

One of the most important functions of a board is to hire the chief executive officer. There are many criteria that boards go through to determine the next CEO. In most circumstances the board has many years to plan for this succession. Even where CEOs die, resign, or are terminated, proper corporate governance dictates that the board have a ready list of internal and external candidates from which to choose. The gender of the CEO is clearly within the control of the board, or will be the next time to change.

C. **Boards directly or indirectly influence the gender composition of the top management team (TMT)**

Ultimately, the CEO hires the top management team. Sometimes the board reserves the right to approve hiring specific candidates to the top management team. Boards, therefore, control not just their own composition but also that of the top management team in a firm.

D. **Boards have greater future choice of new board members from among experienced TMT women**

Top management teams are themselves a significant source of new board members. As boards influence the gender composition of the TMT to be more balanced between women and men they will create more candidates for board membership. This, in turn, will feed back to the boards themselves, which choose their own gender composition. More female and male candidates will mean better choice and quality of directors on boards.

This feedback loop is shown in the diagram below (Figure 8.2).

Many studies examine the importance of gender diversity on boards. These studies have led to a view that a more diverse board will produce better corporate governance. Can we measure the value that corporate governance generates for stakeholders? It probably generates quite significant benefits if done properly, but we do not yet have the ability to fully measure all of the benefits.

Compare this to the known relationship between added gender diversity and improved corporate performance, though it's impossible to look backwards. We will never know whether, had the Bank of America board been more gender diverse in 2008, they would have stopped management from purchasing Merrill Lynch. Similarly, had the Royal Bank of Scotland been more gender diverse at board level, we will never know whether their management would have been prevented from going on a series of reckless acquisitions.

We can never know what might have happened in these examples. However, we can look forward with the knowledge that boards entirely of men can improve in performance with the addition of just one woman member. The cost of substituting qualified women for men on boards and on management is zero and more gender diversity improves performance. What chance do you think there is of a management team being gender diverse if the board is not also gender diverse?

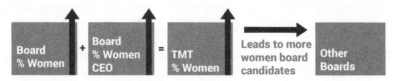

Figure 8.2 Top Management Teams as a Source for Board Members

HUMANS FOLLOW ROLE MODELS

We have been taught to do this since we were children. What more relevant role model could top management teams have than the board of directors? A board composed exclusively of men, or mainly men, signifies very clearly to the top management team that men alone constitute the right pool of candidates for selection to top management. Board members are people who have made it. They have had distinguished careers and are now fit to govern a public company.

It is theoretically possible, of course, that a CEO will choose a gender diverse top management team regardless of the composition of the board. But the available data suggests that this is rarely done. With human nature as it is, influenced to follow the leader, it is unlikely that CEOs would make a change, or challenge the status quo on their own. However, some do and that's why we have male leaders today, gender-intelligent men, effecting change in their organizations and encouraging their boards to follow suit.

ROLE MODELS ARE LEADERS

Gordon Nixon, the president, CEO, and director of Royal Bank of Canada from 2001 to 2014, couldn't tell his board what to do, but as CEO, he could tell management, and the board followed him. In my interview with Gord, he shares the challenges he faced as CEO in bringing greater gender parity to his executive team and how that ultimately influenced the board to become more gender diverse.

The Royal Bank of Canada is known to everyone in the banking world, and one of the reasons is that RBC just happens to be Canada's largest bank. How does RBC score consistently leading marks in gender diversity in the banking industry? We wanted to know. So we called up recently retired CEO Gordon Nixon, and asked if we could visit to chat about what actions he took as CEO of RBC to cause the firm to achieve these leading results. Mr. Nixon was willing to see us, as this was clearly a subject he had embraced and felt others should as well.

Here Is What We Heard in Our Chat

Gordon Nixon was very specific about RBC's approach to gender diversity and shared the following points:

- Gender diversity, and diversity of all kinds, was his priority as well as that of his entire senior management team. The head of human resources was part of this team and she herself was a strong and powerful advocate for gender diversity.
- The diversity committee was made up of senior management from across the firm and membership rotated over time to bring in new managers.

- There were diversity targets set in each business unit. These targets were monitored regularly and were well known within RBC. They were tailored to each business unit by what was achievable from the available workforce.
- There were scorecards and progress was measured four times per year.
- Hard (specific numbers) diversity targets were built in to annual reviews.
- Hiring was an important diversity event. Every senior-level employee had to go through a process to ensure that a full suite of diverse candidates had been considered. Those activities were supervised by an HR department that had real "teeth" in ensuring that the processes were followed.

Mr. Nixon told us that if you measure all levels of management today, women fill 40 percent of the leadership roles at RBC. This bodes well for future senior management candidates to be women and perhaps one day, the CEO.

We have seen many of the practices that were followed at RBC recommended by experts in diversity, and the results speak for themselves. Interestingly, RBC is regularly ranked as one of the best, if not the best performing among Canadian banks. So we have a firm with a standout record in gender diversity and top marks for its performance across a number of financial and other metrics.

Correlations That Count

The more gender diverse the board of directors becomes, the more likely it is that CEOs will respond and hire more women in management. In turn, the top management team of women and men will similarly respond to the signal sent by the board and CEO that gender diversity is important to their company. If this is true then we should be able to find a correlation between the gender diversity of board members and the gender diversity of top management teams, and that's exactly what we find in Canada's leading companies.

Case Study: Canada's S&P/TSX 60 Companies

The S&P/TSX 60 index includes the largest companies by capitalization traded on the Toronto Stock Exchange. The sixty companies represented in the index are a cross section of Canada's largest public companies representing all industries. The makeup of the companies in the index parallels the Canadian equity markets and is strongly weighted to mining, oil and gas, and financial services.

In our research we were able to obtain twelve years of data (2002 to 1014) from the Clarkson Centre at Rotman School of Management on three key variables:

1. Gender of the board chair
2. Gender of the CEO
3. Women and men on the board of directors

In order to complete the regression analysis, we also needed to know the women and men on top management teams for the sixty companies in the S&P/TSX 60 each year back to 2002. These we produced year by year from company reports and filings.

The scarcity of females in either CEO or the chair roles for these sixty companies placed a limit on our analysis. There is only one woman CEO in all of Canada's major companies in the S&P/TSX 60. Congratulations, Transalta Corporation! There are actual two times as many women chairs as there are CEOs, for a total of two chairs across the entire index during this time period.

This limits the usefulness of these variables in determining the correlation of these factors (number of CEO or chairs) with the number of women on the top management team. However, the good news is that we do have data on the number of women on boards and the number of women in top management teams for these sixty companies.

Finally, the composition of the index changes over time. To handle this complication we took the sixty companies as they existed at the end of 2014 and used these same companies' data going back twelve years. If the company was under twelve years old we used only the data available from the company's existence. We ran a number of analyses on this data — and guess what?

A Strong Correlation Exists!

There is a strong positive correlation between the between the percentage of women on a company's board of directors (with a lag of one year) and the percentage of women in their top management team, or TMT. This finding calls for a "eureka moment." We now have a mathematical relationship between board gender composition and the gender composition of the top management team. More women on boards should lead to more women in TMT one year later. So all the work going into adding women to boards is not only the right thing to do but will actually change the leadership teams and the companies themselves.

We see in this analysis that the two levels of governance are directly related to one another. This has important implications for how governance committees should be creating their board's gender composition. We know now that it will have a direct relationship on their management's gender composition.

We also looked at whether we could find a linear regression in the data. We could not find one. In other words, there is not a simple formula that says if you do more of one thing then you will be gaining more of the other thing. This implies that the relationships that arise from gender diversity may be quite complex. For example, what if the effect of women directors on changing the composition of the TMT is weak until there is a critical mass of women directors on the board?

Then the power to influence TMT composition grows for a time while the percentage of women on the board goes up. At some point this effect may be fully exhausted (say, for example, at 50 percent of the board) and adding more women directors will not have a further impact on the composition of the TMT. This could be called a parabolic relationship. This is just speculation, mind you. We will need much more data and research to know exactly how it will work.

For the S&P/TSX 60 companies, we will start to receive more information as a result of the Ontario Securities Commission's new regulations for public companies, which require companies to comply or explain on the gender mix of public company boards. It will open a world of new possibilities to find relationships that companies will be able to put to work to improve the gender diversity of their leadership and the performance of their firms.

WOMEN'S PARTICIPATION IN MANAGEMENT AND ON BOARDS

Women have been making progress in business both at the senior management level and on boards of directors. This has been the subject of a great deal of media interest. We attend many meetings on this subject, where the general conclusion is that women's advancement in management has stalled. Some believe that there has been little increase in the movement of women into management roles over the past decade. This is often used as a reason for more accelerated policy changes such as quotas and additional disclosure.

In most of the world progress has not stopped. We know this because analysis of this topic has substantially improved in the past five years. As mentioned previously, one paper I would recommend for senior executives comes from Credit Suisse's research institute, "CS Gender 3000: Women in Senior Management."

One of their key findings is that diversity has increased in virtually every country in every sector from 2010 to 2013:[15]

- The level of diversity on boards was 9.6 percent in 2010 and increased to 12.7 percent in 2013.
- Women CEOs and women managers reporting to CEOs accounted for 12.9 percent of the total population at the end of 2013. This average varies across countries and between sectors.
- Around the world there's been a drop from 39 to 34 percent in the number of companies without any women on the board of directors.
- Over half of European companies have more than 20 percent women on their boards. This is double the level found in North America.
- Boards with female representation had a dividend payout ratio of 39 percent compared to those without women at 32 percent.
- Companies with more than 50 percent of women in top management had a dividend payout ratio of 43 percent versus only 36 percent dividend payout ratio in companies with less than 10 percent women as top managers.

	US	UK	Canada	Global
Women on Boards - 2010/13	12.7%/13.7%	10.1%/17.9%	12.5%/15.9%	9.6%/12.7%
Women CEO 2013	3.5%	5.1%	2.6%	3.9%
Women in Mgt. 2013	14.8%	15.9%	16.7%	12.9%

Figure 8.3   Women as a Percentage of Corporate Leadership

As shown in Figure 8.3, women now compose 12.9 percent of senior managers globally; however, only 3.9 percent of CEOs around the world are women. Women also make up 12.7 percent of boards globally, with some small variations by industry.[16]

This progress is undeniable, yet it starts from a small base. At this rate it will take many more years, even decades, to achieve some sense of parity of involvement. For some, this progress isn't fast enough and they advocate for both voluntary and regulatory means to speed up the process.

MEN'S BELIEFS AND BEHAVIORS
ARE CHANGING . . . SLOWLY

"Richard, look at all the things corporate leaders say about the advancement of women and diversity in their corporations. Look at what chairs say about their commitment to diversity on their boards; then look at the results. The results are poor versus the lofty goals declared by company leaders. Any other corporate objective with similar resources devoted to it would have achieved substantially more results in the time available."

"It's what you said, Barbara, about the difference between intention and behavior in Chapter 7 and the need for male leaders to find that congruence. There are both men and women who truly believe in this objective and who have made progress within their organizations. However, the majority of men running corporations today must, to judge by their actions, believe that their companies would not be better if they had promoted women into management roles and their boards over the past decade.

"Richard, our book is intended to inflate men's passion and commitment. Every aspect of our book is a call for men to act on gender diversity and the advancement of women into leadership.

"We've shared the business case for the advancement of women and the neuroscience that underlies our gender differences and accentuates the power of our complement. We spoke of the ascent of women in education and leadership across the globe and the ascent of men, committed to the concept that women are able to lead in any capacity.

"There are increasingly more men today—at the board and executive levels—who are steadfast in bringing more women into leadership roles because they know it will improve the innovation, productivity, and financial performance of their organizations."

ENDNOTES

1. Jena McGregor, "The Boardroom Is Still an Old Boy's Club," *The Washington Post*, September 25, 2013, https://www.washingtonpost.com/news/on-leadership/wp/2013/09/25/corporate-boardrooms-are-still-old-boys-clubs/.

2. Ibid.

3. Ibid.

4. Ibid.

5. Madeline Meth, "Women's Leadership: What's True, What's False, and Why It Matters," Center for American Progress report, March 2014, 5, https://cdn.americanprogress.org/wp-content/uploads/2014/03/WomensLeadership-report.pdf.

6. Evan Apfelbaum, "What's the Business Case for Diversity in the Workplace?"

7. Agnes Bolsø and Siri Øyslebø Sørensen, "How the Quota Law Came About: A Brief Overview," Department of Interdisciplinary Studies of Culture, Norwegian University of Science and Technology, presentation at the conference Women on Company Boards: How Norway Uses Quotas, January 23, 2013, House of Commons, London, http://www.ntnu.edu/documents/32998871/33046696/Made+in+Norway/413070eb-dc21-4413-ba09-cccb73be6074.

8. Ibid.

9. Scott E. Page, *The Difference: How the Power of Diversity Creates Better Groups, Firms, Schools, and Societies* (Princeton, NJ: Princeton University Press, 2008), 323.

10. Ibid., 352.

11. Ibid., 357.

12. Brenda Hoffman, senior vice president, head of global technology, U.S. Markets Systems and Global Information Services, Nasdaq, in a discussion with Richard Nesbitt, August 2016.

13. James Kristie, "Say It Ain't So: 'Parsley on Fish,'" *Boards at Their Best: Insights on Leadership and Corporate Governance* (blog), March 31, 2009, http://jameskristie.blogspot.com/2009/03/say-it-aint-so-parsley-on-fish.html.

14. John Schnatter, "Where Were the Boards: Accountability Shouldn't End with the CEO," *Wall Street Journal*, October 25, 2008, http://www.wsj.com/articles/SB122489049222968569.

15. Richard Kersley, Michael O' Sullivan, "CS Gender 3000: Women in Senior Management," Credit Suisse Research Institute, September 2014, https://publications.credit-suisse.com/tasks/render/file/index.cfm?fileid=812 8F3C0-99BC-22E6-838E2A5B1E4366DF.

16. Ibid.

Chapter 9

MEASURING COMMITMENT

"Whether we run countries or companies, we simply cannot afford to leave half our team sitting on the bench."
— Kathleen Taylor, Former President and CEO,
Four Seasons Hotels and Resorts

"Barbara, this was Katie Taylor summing it up during my interview with her in February 2016. Her story of her ascent in leadership is back in Chapter 2, but it was her additional comments on the commitment of men that I felt were appropriate here in Chapter 9. She went on to explain whom she meant was benching half the team."

Men play a key role in changing the paradigm. By an overwhelming majority, men occupy the CEO suite and board chair positions, and it is they who are responsible in that same majority for setting strategic direction and managing talent development and succession planning at senior levels. It follows, therefore, that it is the personal commitment and accountability of these leaders—to drive a focus on diversity and inclusion—that will be the key to generating change.[1]

"Richard, Katie has certainly faced many challenges on her path to becoming the chair of the largest bank in Canada. It's often a challenge for women to practice their own authentic style of leadership and be valued for their contribution; it's also a challenge for men to recognize that value and embrace the complementary nature that women bring to business.

"Investors would love to own a company that generates superior performance. Shareholders would also appreciate it. Employees and job candidates seek out such companies. Governments appreciate the higher tax revenues that are generated. All of society benefits from greater innovation and a better environmental record. It seems clear that stakeholders want superior performance.

"You and I both know that the evidence on how to generate superior performance has been known and documented for the past twenty years. In fact, Dr. Roy Adler began his longitudinal studies in the early 1980s. The preponderance of the data says that adding women to boards and management improves corporate performance. The more diverse you are, the better your performance will become. We've presented a lot of that evidence in this book."

In the previous chapter, we demonstrated a statistical correlation between the number of women on a company's board and the number of women on the top management team. We allowed for a time lag of one year for this correlation to manifest itself, which makes sense. One year allows a CEO to respond to a major change in the gender diversity of the board. This important finding helps to justify the work being done today by different groups to examine the number of women on boards. It should also lead us to question why these boards are not even more gender diverse.

Now we want to share a model we developed that will enable us to evaluate public data to see if we can predict whether a company is more or less likely to add women as directors, or hire more women into management. In Chapter 2, we gave readers the supporting evidence to show that gender diversity on boards affects the bottom line, and showed how board diversity helps to promote diversity in senior management.

A GENERAL MODEL FOR GENDER DIVERSITY IN MANAGEMENT INFORMATION SYSTEMS (MIS)

Successful managers crave information. One of the key determinants of a successful strategy is the ability to deliver management information on time and with sufficient granularity to enable management to act, changing moderate success into superb outcomes or preventing unexpected failures. If you are the senior executive tasked with developing and implementing strategies to improve gender diversity and company performance, you will need information and you will also be required to provide information to others.

As we noted earlier, over the past twenty years, substantial research has accumulated to demonstrate a strong correlation between companies that embrace diversity and those that enjoy superior corporate performance. Some of the actions aimed at promoting gender diversity on the boards of public companies and in senior management positions can be measured through publicly available information. We can use evidence of action to infer the probable intent of the company's leaders regarding gender diversity.

This will permit comparison of companies both within and across sectors. Because research almost unanimously supports the strong correlation between an increase in gender diversity and superior corporate performance, this measurement may also predict future performance.

In order to develop a general model of gender diversity in corporations, we first need to define our territory. So let's start with some basic assumptions:

- Organizations are hierarchical.
- In most cases, an employee's objective is to be promoted to more senior roles in order to achieve higher compensation, status, greater span of control, and so forth.
- When staffing roles, organizations may either promote from within, which is usually the case, or recruit new employees from elsewhere, via the labor market.
- The percentage of women in entry-level roles should reflect labor market gender demographics for people qualified for and interested in these roles, provided discrimination is not present.
- The percent of women at level M+1 should reflect level M (the lower level), provided discrimination is not present (where M is the management level under consideration). For example, the percentage of women at the vice president (V) level should not be materially different than the percentage of women at the director (D) level.
- The CEO can be a man or a woman.
- There is no incentive for a firm to create false signals about gender diversity as the cost incurred from discovery of these false signals would exceed any benefit.
- No company would produce an auditable signal of commitment to gender diversity if an audit could determine this signal is actually false.
- No company would submit false signals to be audited.

So, with these fundamental assumptions let's see how we can develop a model to measure commitment to change.

DEFINING A MODEL FOR GENDER DIVERSITY

The basic hierarchical model of a typical corporation is generally well accepted. Figure 9.1 depicts a six-level corporation from the board of directors at the top, through various management layers, to entry-level employees at the base of this structure. If the gender mix between employees becomes imbalanced at any level, a company has the option to hire from a large external pool of potential employees and should therefore be able to fill positions as required.

We could start to build our model by measuring and reporting the fraction of women employees (n women) / (n men + n women) for each of the six levels we've identified. This will create six different fractions representing the number of women as a percentage of total employees at each level. These figures will

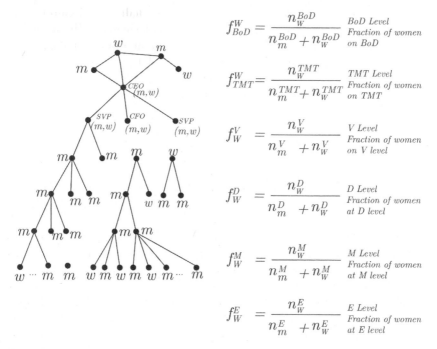

Figure 9.1   Gender Diversity Index—Model and Analytics

provide management with a measure for gender diversity status at a single point in time for each level.

The next step is to make pairwise comparisons between these fractions at different levels. For example, we can compare manager level to board of directors level, the director level versus the vice president level, the top management team (TMT) level versus the board of director level (D level in Figure 9.1) and so on. This will result in fifteen pairwise comparisons as shown in Figure 9.2. Knowing these fifteen results will give management access to powerful data.

Pairwise comparisons can be used to define how many women, as a fraction of total employees whom management wants to have at a particular level. It is also possible to gain insight through making meaningful comparisons between levels, looking inside the company's management structure to find out exactly where the "glass ceiling" (a situation where gender progress is blocked) or the "leaky pipe" (where gender progress is reduced as women exit the firm) is having its greatest impact.

For example, if you have 50 percent women at the vice president level and 0 percent at the top management team (TMT) level (an impermeable glass ceiling), it would indicate a need to focus senior management's attention to address this issue at this level and all levels in between. If each successive level has a

(1) Proportions of women at different hierarchical levels (between 4 and 6)

$$\left[f_W^{BoD}, CEO_W, f_W^{TMT}, f_W^{V}, f_W^{D}, f_W^{M}, f_W^{E} \right]$$

Use ratio tests

$$f_W^{E} \gtrsim f_W^{M}$$

$$f_W^{M} \gtrsim f_W^{V}$$

$$f_W^{V} \gtrsim f_W^{TMT}$$

$$f_W^{TMT} \gtrsim f_W^{M} \ \cdots$$

$$\cdots$$

(2) Signals:
- Gender diversity policy: private/public;
- Auditable: yes/no;
- Audited: yes/no, private/public

(3) Industry variables:
- Grad rates, women f_W^{Grad} : sets baseline

6 variables generate 15 performance indicators via comparisons of proportion of women at different hierarchical levels

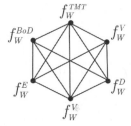

Figure 9.2 Variables to Be Disclosed/Measured

lower fraction of women than the previous level, this may reflect a systemic "leaky pipe" problem. Company-wide solutions would be required for this problem at all levels.

"Imagine, Barbara, if a CEO or an EVP of gender diversity had this information. He or she would be able to pinpoint where these problems are located, and then come up with action plans targeted to resolve them.

"This is far more powerful than a generic statement that a company supports gender diversity. While many companies claim to have this kind of information, and all companies should be able to generate it, this kind of data is rarely made public."

"Richard, they may claim they have this information, but many do not track the representation or retention of women at various management levels. This targeted approach would be a huge value to companies looking to get the most out of their gender diversity initiatives. They can design programs that address the changing landscape of challenges that women may face at different rungs of the corporate ladder.

"For example, in Chapter 7, we explain that work-life flexibility programs are an excellent recruitment strategy because they're of great value to many women at entry and mid-management levels. The problem is, these programs are of little to no value to women at the stage in their lives when they are looking to advance to senior positions.

"So, when you ask company leaders, 'What are you trying to solve for through your gender diversity programs?,' the common response is to increase the representation of women at the executive level, and they hold up programs such as work-life flexibility as a panacea, when its value is real, but limited in effectiveness. There are many programs that fall into these blind spots that we will cover in Chapter 10."

Meaningful change is not likely to happen unless firms are committed to generating this kind of data, making it publicly available and—perhaps most important—providing enough information to parties with the mandate and power to be able to act on it.

We now have fifteen variables that we can measure to develop a model of gender diversity performance at a given point in time. As we take successive readings of these pairwise comparisons, we develop a picture of how the company is trending in its gender diversity performance. This is tremendously valuable in determining a company's progress in and commitment to gender diversity on boards and in management.

GENDER DIVERSITY MODEL FOR MANAGEMENT INFORMATION SYSTEM (MIS)

Many experts in this field have recommended certain variables that can be used as predictive signals to understand a company's approach to gender diversity. If you combine these with the general model described in the previous section, the following measurable and publicly available factors can be used to inform a gender diversity MIS data set.

The first three criteria are board-specific decisions made by boards on the nature of the board composition from a gender perspective.

Is the Chair a Man or a Woman?

The research is unclear about the impact of the chair's gender. It seems logical that this is a factor that should be measured. Future work can determine its significance.

Is the CEO a Man or a Woman?

As the leader, the CEO has the most impact on the organization. Research indicates that companies with female CEOs have more women in executive positions. This fact helps to promote the advancement of women in the organization.

What Percentage of the Board Are Women?

Research indicates that board diversity makes for stronger boards. There is a correlation between women on boards and the number of women in top management teams. Research has highlighted key strengths that women bring to boards.

The next two criteria are management specific and are decisions that are under the CEO's control, and reflect decisions they have made on the diversity composition of their top management team.

What Percentage of the TMT Are Women?

Research indicates that female executives significantly influence both a company's culture and its decision making. Having more women in management leads to enhanced performance, which creates a positive impact on businesses' corporate results and ultimately increases shareholder value.

What Percentage of Women Are in Power Roles on the TMT?

Power roles—such as chief financial officer, chief risk officer, and business heads—are positions of real influence. The other roles in the top management team, such as human resources, legal, and public affairs, are referred to as shared services. The sphere of influence and potential for the progression of female leaders are inhibited by a severe skewing in roles away from the CEO and operational roles to that of shared services.

> "Richard, the percentage of women in power roles on the top management team is a critical criteria to measure. Women may represent one of five positions in senior management globally, but when we look more closely (see Figure 9.3), they continue to be centralized in management support functions rather than in strategic leadership roles."

> "A huge assumption out there is that women are not putting themselves up for promotion or for the 'P&L assignments' that will give them the experience and prominence necessary for advancement to senior leadership. Men need to see women in these strategic leadership roles and be active in mentoring and advocating for women in power roles.

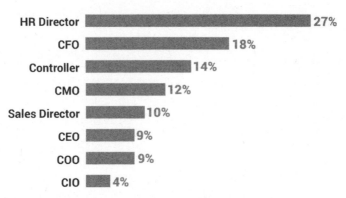

Figure 9.3 Women's Roles in Senior Management

"In Chapter 7, we spoke of the need to have male leadership out in front, personally committed, and leading the transformation. Affecting the percentage of women in power roles on the TMT is what this is all about. Companies are accomplishing this through male sponsorship, a gender-intelligent lens placed on new talent management, and succession planning programs."

These next two criteria are specific elements of disclosure, which indicate a company's attitude toward gender diversity in the management and governance of the firm.

Gender Progress Disclosure

Transparency demonstrates commitment and conviction. If a company is willing to make a statement with regards to its gender diversity goal, then it is more likely to pursue diversity, as compared with a company that doesn't make such a public statement.

Gender Diversity Targets

It is important to share this kind of information within the company and make it publicly available because progress creates progress. This type of progress can also help senior leaders to maintain focus and enthusiasm.

The final two criteria describe the way a company has designed its processes, both board and management, to produce the desired result of more (or less) gender diversity.

Gender Diversity Statement

This is a statement made publicly and regularly by the CEO or chair stating the firm's support for improving gender diversity on the board, TMT, and throughout the management structure.

Board Selection Process

Does the board selection process consider gender? The board nominating committee should be formally required to consider gender targets in its selection process.

Each of these categories of criteria describes the relative importance that the firm's leadership has placed on current and future levels of gender diversity. If a company has no activities supporting any one of the criteria, then management has determined that diversity is not important to them. If the company does not disclose that it is carrying on such activities, it can be assumed that the company does not think these factors are important to its strategy.

Conversely, if a firm proudly discloses its diversity activity against a defined set of criteria and that disclosure is robust, then we can conclude that the company is actively seeking change and working toward that change.

Are there other criteria we would like to measure? Yes there are. But most of these are currently nonpublic and are known only to a company's management and boards or, in a worst-case scenario, not known at all. It is a company's responsibility to demonstrate its intentions on gender diversity and provide as much public information as possible.

The following are the factors that we would use, if they were all available, to determine a company's commitment to gender diversity, both in terms of present and probable future behavior:

1. Percentage of women at each level of organization—six levels as in the previous example
2. Chair—woman or man
3. CEO—woman or man
4. Percentage of board made up of women
5. Differential for each point at each level (fifteen points noted above)
6. Top management team (TMT) percentage of women
7. Qualified women in workforce (available for recruitment or not readily available)
8. Public diversity policy (available yes/no)
9. Public diversity targets (available yes/no)
10. Gender progress disclosure and audit of this report

Secret Campaigns to Increase Gender Diversity Will Not Be Successful

Simply put, "secret" gender diversity campaigns are not effective. The reasons should be obvious: but in case they aren't, let's go over them here. Many stakeholders will want to know that a company supports gender diversity. They need to know how deeply the company is committed to it and timelines for action to take place. This information is important to many stakeholders: from various levels of management, employees, and candidates thinking about joining the firm, to investors, clients, and suppliers. Conceptually we could examine the following (possible responses are given in brackets):

- Does the company have a gender diversity policy that is public and is specific enough to measure? [Yes or No]
- Is the gender diversity policy auditable in that it contains targets or quotas? [Yes or No]
- Is this gender diversity policy actually audited? If so, are these auditing results made public? (Note: submitting this information in required regulatory filing makes it both audited and public.) [Private or public, internal or external]

"Richard, one of the top reasons companies do not divulge their gender diversity campaigns is so as not to broadcast that they have a 'women-in-leadership' problem. It took the technology industry years to own up to the fact that it has a problem recruiting and retaining women.

"Transparency is a move in the right direction but it's still not the solution. For instance, Intel was one of the first tech companies to make their diversity numbers public over ten years ago, but the ratio of men to women hasn't changed since 2010. And the other tech companies have made some progress since they started to disclose their gender diversity numbers in 2014, but only marginally."[2]

CONSTRUCTING A NEW GENDER PROPENSITY INDEX©

The research we have referenced may be very interesting, but readers might fairly ask how we go about creating something that can be used by stakeholders, such as investors or prospective employees. Don't stakeholders want to know about a company's gender diversity policies? Wouldn't they want to know how strongly management advocates for these policies and then puts this commitment into action?

Similarly, wouldn't stakeholders be interested in knowing about companies that perform well in this regard, or companies that do not consider these factors sufficiently important to place appropriate weight on them in their decision-making process?

The answer to all of these questions is: yes. Institutional investors, employees, potential employees, families of employees and potential employees, analysts, retail shareholders, governments, and regulators are just some of the stakeholders who have a real and passionate interest in how public companies respond to the challenge of improving performance.

When faced with large quantities of data, one means of better understanding it is to consolidate the data into a single numerical output or score, such as an index. Stock market indices are an example of these. They reflect a shortcut that can be used to access desired information, usually for comparison purposes.

For example, how did equity markets perform today versus yesterday? How well did a company do versus the index?

In assessing a set of gender diversity factors, we can use the same technique, turning each piece of data into a component part of the index. Adopting this approach enables us to create a mathematical relationship for the variable factor with other variable factors. For example, let's say we are looking at whether the CEO is a woman or a man.

Whereas there may be some debate about whether weightings are correct, and how best to use this information, we argue that the ideal use of this index is not the specific number output, but what happens over time at each of the companies being examined. Does the index change over time? Does it get higher (better) or worse (lower)? Can we see any relationship between these scores and a company's financial performance over the next several years? Is there a correlation between the index and future financial performance?

Given that this is a new field, there will inevitably be more questions than answers. We therefore caution readers not to make too much of the index itself. Instead, we believe discussion should focus on the benefits that can be obtained from this information and its usefulness as a tool to help achieve gender success at each company, to the benefit of all stakeholders.

Before we receive lots of calls from investor relation officers, we hope each company reflects on the work they are doing to shift the gender composition of their leadership. If the GPI$^{©}$ score of your firm is high, then congratulations. If the score is low, then all of these items are in your control and we could see you back next year with a better score if you take action.

A company's GPI can be improved if that company adjusts any one of the nine variables to strengthen its commitment to gender diversity while maintaining the other variables at a constant level. This will increase their GPI score and send a message to stakeholders that gender diversity has become a more important factor at the company.

Of course, companies can also choose to ignore their GPI results. In this case, companies that have low scores and do not seek to improve should perform less well financially over time than peers that do seek to increase their GPI and benefit from it. As we said in an earlier chapter, everyone can choose to believe or disbelieve the results of research.

You can choose to believe the experts who agree that these factors are important in the gender makeup of your firm's leadership. Everyone can choose to act or not, to reap the opportunities that come with gender diversity in leadership and governance of companies, or fail to do so. The research presented here suggests that companies that take action will show significant improvement in their corporate performance across a broad range of measures.

WHAT HAPPENS NEXT?

In the year ahead, more information on companies' activities will be amassed to prove that improving gender diversity on boards and management generates superior corporate performance. Some of that information will be provided thanks to existing and forthcoming regulations. Even more information may come because company leaders realize that providing this information is in their company's best interests. The Gender Propensity Index will continue to evolve as more information becomes available.

We stand on the edge of dramatic progress in the ongoing evolution of business. Investors are starting to take note of those who make most effective use of the full pool of human resources available, tapping into an immensely talented group of star performers. Similarly, regulators and government have found the current pace of change to be too slow and have been discussing a number of new techniques to accelerate this change.

"Barbara, I don't believe these heavy-handed approaches should be necessary. As we've cited several times in this book, compliance is not the solution, especially if our goal is to convince men to become more actively involved in the advancement of women into leadership.

"Market forces are providing the solution by offering economic rewards for gender diversity. That will have more influence on male leaders than government regulations and forced quotas ever could hope to have. A growing number of male leaders are beginning to recognize that now and even more so in the future, success will require hiring more women at all levels of a firm and advancing them into management."

"Richard, that's why a growing number of men who run companies, the 20 percent of male leaders that we spoke of in Chapter 5 who get it and are doing something about it, have perceived the benefit in changing their approach to gender diversity. They've become champions of change. And I agree that their success and outspoken advocacy will have a greater effect on the 60 percent of men who are believers, but looking for direction.

"Identifying what works and what doesn't, as we did in Chapter 7, provides excellent direction for men and women in leadership positions about which gender diversity programs to focus on and get behind. Chapter 10 will provide even more direction by identifying the systems, processes, and procedures in companies—what you call the 'plumbing'—that can potentially harbor systemic biases. To continue with your metaphor: those need to be flushed clean of any obstructions or blockages to women's advancement!"

ENDNOTES

1. Kathleen Taylor, former president and CEO, Four Seasons Hotels and Resorts, in a discussion with Richard Nesbitt, September, 2016
2. Sarah Kessler, "Tech's Big Gender Diversity Push, One Year In," *Fast Company*, November 19, 2015, http://www.fastcompany.com/3052877/techs-big-gender-diversity-push-one-year-in.

Chapter 10

HOW TO RID THE PLUMBING OF BIAS

"Barbara, I've been using the word 'plumbing' for a few years now as a metaphor for flushing out the systemic bias—both seen and unseen—that prevents women from advancing and succeeding in leadership. There are other metaphors that could work just as well, but 'plumbing' works for me on two levels: we are always speaking of talent pipelines, and plumbing itself is something that men can understand and appreciate.

"'Plumbing' refers to the systems, processes, and procedures within the company that affect the intake, evaluation, promotion, and ultimate retention of employees. Every business has plumbing of some sort. Common to all plumbing systems is the presence of one source of fresh water in and one source of wastewater out. The journey in between is what makes life bearable. Get the plumbing right and life is luxurious. Get it wrong and life can be unbearable and sometimes downright dangerous."

"Richard, I want you to win! 'Plumbing' works for me. In our work at the Gender Intelligence Group, we use the word 'lever.' The word comes from the French *lever*, meaning 'to raise'; we think of the initiatives and actions crucial for bringing about change and transforming cultures as *levers* that leaders and organizations raise. Put the correct levers in place and they become the key elements underlying the transformation—a fresh water system!

"We've identified nine such levers that we will share later on in this chapter and show how well they strengthen what works in gender diversity and, to borrow again from your metaphor, flush out what doesn't."

In corporations, all of the systems, procedures, formal and informal interaction, hierarchies, and communication methods are a form of corporate plumbing. Companies invest a great deal of resources in their plumbing. However, just as with the plumbing in a house, sometimes it does not deliver the result one desires.

Inputs come into the company, rattle around through systems and processes, and then exit the company as outputs. But sometimes they may not follow the path you want them to follow or produce what you expected. In companies (unlike houses), there may not be any leaks or flooded basements as evidence, so people keep using the same plumbing system over and over, which continues to deliver the same non-optimal result. Getting it right will make success significantly easier than having to produce results in spite of bad plumbing.

GENDER PARITY IN NEW GRADUATES

Let us give you an example. A company sets a target of gender parity for their intake of new graduates this year. That's right: 50 percent women and 50 percent men. HR sends the recruitment team off to universities to recruit, but they return with candidate recommendations that are not fifty-fifty.

The company has a closer look. It turns out the recruitment committee itself was 90 percent men and 10 percent women and they only went to two universities, the two they always visit for recruitment efforts. They visited only one faculty department that has a gender composition of 30 percent women and 70 percent men. The chosen entertainment at the recruitment social event was male-oriented. Their conclusion was that there were not sufficient women candidates, so the market solution was to hire the men available.

This is a very common approach to recruitment. Of course you can see the problems with this approach. The plumbing is inherently biased toward finding male candidates. It has been the practice for as long as anyone can remember, so why change it?

SOURCING, JOB DESCRIPTIONS, AND INTERVIEWING

There are three specific areas in most companies of narrow thinking and unconscious bias in the recruitment and interviewing process: sourcing, job posting, and interviewing.

Sourcing

Many leaders and organizations focus on discipline-specific pools of candidates and often compete with others for the same talent. We often hear, "There just aren't enough women in the industry. Sourcing challenges occur more frequently in engineering, technology, investment, and capital markets." Yet, there are companies who are applying Gender Intelligence to their sourcing and interviewing process.

An investment firm in Boston was having trouble recruiting women as financial advisors. Their target for years had been female business school graduates and the field was thin. They began recruiting women in the field of education, where 90 percent of graduates are women. They also recruited women graduates in pharmacology, where near 70 percent of graduates are women. Although women have high graduation rates, there simply aren't enough jobs in these fields. Smart move on the part of the investment firm, though. They realized that women graduating from these two fields (and there are probably many others) have critical thinking skills. The firm's financial products and services can easily be taught. They recruited nine women and six of them turned out to be huge successes as financial advisors.

We're seeing the same thing in technology. One of the largest ERPs in the world is recruiting more women from pharmaceutical sales to sell software. They realize that critical thinking is the skill they need. And just as the investment firm and many other companies are concluding, they can always teach the software.

IT leaders, such as Brenda Hoffman at NASDAQ (her story is in Chapter 6), are looking for women technologists with degrees, skills, and experience in fields such as law, literature, and even anthropology to provide what she calls "EQ programming"—the emotional quotient connection for the competitive advantage in unique user interface experiences.

- Mining and oil and gas industry companies are creating "talent supply chains" from high schools and universities into their companies. Their intent is to encourage young girls to pursue degrees in STEM.

  Women leaders in the companies become role models by visiting schools and presenting engineering as a fulfilling profession and encouraging young girls with interests in engineering to pursue those interests. Internships that begin in high school and college often directly lead to employment.

Job Posting

Gender bias exists in the language that companies use in job descriptions, company profiles, websites, and other social media. We touched on this in Chapter 7 but will delve a little deeper here.

Research shows that women job seekers were more interested in male-dominated jobs when advertisements were unbiased. For example, women and men may equally desire an engineering position, but highly masculine wording used in the posting reduces the job's appeal to women. The language signals that women may not fit or belong. In this way, qualified female—and some male applicants—are opting out of jobs in which they could have otherwise performed well.

Male-themed words used in an engineering job description[1]

Company Description	We are a *dominant* engineering firm that *boasts* many *leading* clients. We are *determined* to *stand apart* from the *competition*.
Qualifications	*Strong* communication and *influencing* skills. Ability to *perform individually* in a *competitive* environment. *Superior* ability to *satisfy* customers and manage company's association with them.
Responsibilities	*Direct* project groups to *manage* project *progress* and ensure accurate task *control. Determine compliance* with client's *objectives*.

Female-themed words used in an engineering job description[2]

Company Description	We are a *community* of engineers who have effective *relationships* with many *satisfied* clients. We are *committed* to *understanding* the engineer sector *intimately*.
Qualifications	*Proficient* oral and written communications skills. Collaborates well in a *team* environment. *Sensitive* to clients' needs, can *develop warm* client *relationships*.
Responsibilities	Provide general *support* to project team in a manner *complimentary* to the company. *Help* clients with construction *activities*.

Job descriptions, the language used on company websites, and images depicting women in leadership positions play a critical role in recruiting female talent, and often provide the first impression of the organization's culture.

According to the study from the *Journal of Personality and Social Psychology* on gendered wording in job advertisements, making these adjustments toward feminine word choices had little effect on the men in terms of dissuading them from applying.[3] Their word scanning tends to focus on tangibles such as salary and position.

Interviewing

Men and women differ in how they prepare for the interview, how they respond to questions, and how they speak of their strengths and weaknesses. Remember the bell curve of gender tendencies we used in Chapter 3? It applies to the interviewing process as well, as described in Figure 10.1.

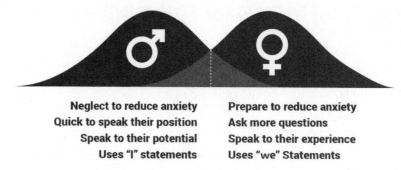

Neglect to reduce anxiety   **Prepare to reduce anxiety**
Quick to speak their position   **Ask more questions**
Speak to their potential   **Speak to their experience**
Uses "I" statements   **Uses "we" Statements**

Figure 10.1   Gender Tendencies During the Interview Process

"Richard, it's very interesting to observe patterns of gender behavior in the interview process. Our research shows that men will often delay preparing for or even thinking about the interview. It's their way of reducing stress. Women, however, tend to prepare and will even go as far as practice interviewing with a friend.

"Ask a man his weakness, and his tendency will be to say, 'I work too much.' It may be a complaint, but men tend to guard and often hide their feelings. It may be a veiled effort to show how strong, competent, or successful they are. Ask a woman her weakness, and her tendency is to say, 'I'm not so strong at analysis,' to show truth about her perceived weakness.

"A guy will claim expertise on something with only a fraction of the skill to do it and with next to no experience, and then they will find a way to do it or learn on the job. Women with equal or better the skill and experience will often hold back from making the same bold statements."

Good interviewers will detect those differences between male and female interviewees. Interviewers who are rushed, scripted, or looking for ease in hiring will not detect them, and that includes both men and women interviewers. Yes, female interviewers can harbor the same biases as male interviewers against women candidates. There are several reasons:

- Interviewers typically assess candidates through a male-oriented paradigm—from style of work to leadership traits.
- They tend to view women candidates who are behaving more in a "female" way as lacking potential and assertiveness.
- The other side of the coin is they also tend to view women who are behaving more in a "male" way as being overly aggressive.
- Often, the business unit leader indicates what he or she is looking for in the character and personality of the candidates and thus the traditional alpha-male model of decision making or sales is seen as the only key success factor.

NINE LEVERS FOR CREATING GENDER-INTELLIGENT ORGANIZATIONS

As we mentioned at the onset of this chapter, there are nine levers, or initiatives and actions, crucial for bringing about change and transforming cultures—what we identify as gender-intelligent organizations. These key elements reveal and correct the many forms of systemic bias. They infuse Gender Intelligence into the leadership style of its executives and managers and into the culture of their teams. The levers reach far into the organization's functions, processes, and systems and result in higher levels of recruitment, engagement, retention, advancement, and productivity. In the following sections you will find a brief description of each.

1. Make Gender Intelligence a Strategic Imperative of the Organization

Treat women in leadership as a compelling business case that even the most cynical observer can buy into. Making Gender Intelligence a strategic imperative of the organization brands the advancement of women a top strategic priority because of its positive impact on the bottom line of the company.

2. Show Conduct and Character Exemplary of a Gender-Intelligent Leader

Conduct gender-intelligent leadership 360s or embed Gender Intelligence into the company's 360 evaluations. Create annual leadership reviews with embedded Gender Intelligence criteria and provide Gender Intelligence leadership coaching for leaders.

3. Embed Gender Intelligence in Hiring Processes

Analyze the hiring practices of the organization for unconscious bias in sourcing, recruiting, and interviewing. Provide the insights and tools to HR interviewers on how to hire gender-intelligent men and women and provide those same tools and insights to managers of business units looking to hire based on an explicitly or implicitly stated set of criteria.

4. Embed Gender Intelligence in Talent Management

Create gender-intelligent meritocracies where the performance standards are based on how men *and* women uniquely think and act to be truly performance based and reflected in evaluations, promotions, succession planning, and candidate leadership training and development.

5. Declare Your Intention to Be a Leading Gender-Intelligent Organization

Internally, portray women leaders in various roles, not just as role models for women, but for male leaders as well. Externally, communicate that the organization encourages and supports young women considering careers in the industry. Organize annual media-attended gender diversity summits with speakers, suppliers, partners, and so forth, that declare the intent of the organization and the quest for gender diverse talent.

6. Generate a Strong Female Leadership Pipeline

Using engineering and technology as an example, develop an internship program for women pursuing engineering degrees, inspiring and empowering high school girls interested in STEM—then intern them into the organization during their college years. Use social media to attract women in middle management who are currently in the industry and looking for a more collaborative and inclusive working environment.

7. Provide Support, Guidance, and Leadership Training for Women

Focus on training for women that identifies and removes any potential pitfalls, such as how to be more self-initiating in navigating their careers; declare their abilities; speak to their potential and not just experience; and practice less self-scrutiny. Measure the satisfaction level of targeted women who participate in the training.

8. Infuse Gender-Intelligent Understanding and Behaviors Internally

Promote Gender Intelligence training for managers to deepen cultural change. Leaders, in particular the CEO and executive committee, must walk the talk and guide by example. Such leaders show greater congruence between intentions and behaviors.

9. Embed Gender Intelligence in All Client/Customer–Facing Efforts

Recognize that clients want to be seen as gender diverse and want to know that their industry partners are also focused on gender diversity. Discover how Gender Intelligence can enhance client-facing efforts. Train both men and women in gender-intelligent selling and client relationship building.

Once an organization has adopted the levers as guiding principles, it becomes easier to (1) identify the usual sources where one may find bias in the plumbing, and (2) create ways in which companies can change their practices to a more gender-balanced approach.

AREAS WHERE SYSTEMIC BIASES MAY FORM

There are a number of areas in an organization where built-in preconceptions and predispositions prevent advancing women into leadership and creating greater gender balance on teams:

- **Benefits programs.** Human resource department should examine all policies under the direction of the gender diversity officer.
- **Uncompetitive or unacceptable maternity leave benefits and practices.** Assign a different manager to be responsible for the retention of each professional maternity leave employee. This manager is to be in regular contact with the employee and to assist her in reintegration back into the firm. This will be part of the manager's evaluation for the period.
- **Incorrect mandate and lopsided gender composition of graduate intake teams.** Closely examine the actions of these teams to ensure they are consistent with an unbiased approach to intake. Look at their actions with potential employees, their recruitment materials, and how they conduct themselves in actual interactions.
- **New hires from both outside the firm and promotions** to new roles within the firm must formally document the candidates considered, including the gender of the candidate. Searches that do not involve acceptable levels of diversity should be rejected and completed again.
- **Broaden the source of new graduates and other new employees** to include other disciplines and other geographies looking for new employees who have a record of achievement and effort.
- **Incorrect mandate and lopsided gender composition of promotion committees.** Top management should examine the promotion committee procedures, recommendations, and their record of the type of promotions they have recommended in the past. Additional information should be examined on how well past-promoted employees have performed.
- **Conduct of management must show the appropriate respect for all employees.** Ongoing training of management to ensure that unintentional or intentional bias is recognized and eliminated from the conduct of managers.
- **Celebrate role models on a gender-diverse basis.** Make certain both female and male models exist for all to see.
- **Succession planning** must be conducted in a gender diverse environment and with expectation that candidates will be gender diverse.

"Barbara, we used to send company representatives out to the business schools to recruit the best and brightest talent we could find. Mainly, it was men going out and they would typically host a reception at the business school and invite young men and women to attend. What was reported back to me by our HR department was that women would come to the doorway of the reception room, they would look around, and they wouldn't enter. They would just turn around and leave. Women HR representatives followed a few to the elevators and asked why they didn't want to go into the reception area and they said they simply didn't feel relaxed or comfortable. They didn't offer much more than that.

"The men that we would send from the company had created this atmosphere that was not conducive to women coming into the room. That story stuck with me. I remember when my HR representative reported this to me and I said, 'That's kind of counterproductive, isn't it? How can we change this?' And we did change."

JUST GO IN THERE

"Reminds me, Richard, of Jennifer Maki, the CEO and executive director of Vale Canada, a Brazilian multinational corporation engaged in metals and mining and one of the largest logistics operators in Brazil. She was part of a CEO network in her industry, yet she hated going to the meetings.[4]

"I asked, 'Why? You have an important voice and there's so much sharing of ideas and thoughts with other leaders. I would bet there are valuable ideas there for your company.'

"'Barbara,' she said, 'It's all men there and maybe one or two women trying so hard to fit in. I felt so uncomfortable as soon as I walked into the room. All I wanted to do was leave. There were a lot of men there to get *their* ideas across and show how much *they* know and it was just boring and I didn't want to hear it anymore.'"

"Barbara, from a male perspective, it's a privilege to be a part of that group. Men would fight and die to be invited to join that network!"

"That's it in a nutshell, Richard. Men tend to be in it for the destination while women join networks and derive just as much value from the journey as well as the outcome.

"Men naturally like to gauge, measure, and compete. I often suggest to male leaders that they put that competiveness aside for a moment and watch and listen. I also suggest that men spend more time being interested and to not try so hard to be interesting."

"Barbara, I would tell women to engage. *Just go in there*. Go into the group or the clique and engage in the business. Partner up with one of the CEOs. You know, many men don't like that constant competition of ideas either. Remember, 20 percent of men get it. Seek out those male CEOs and sit with them during the meetings. Surround yourself with those who think as you do. Don't assume it's hopeless and don't quit. Extract what you need to succeed."

HAVING A HARD TIME GETTING WOMEN TO JOIN

"It happens everywhere, Richard, even in the dean's council at one of the top universities in the northwestern United States. It's a real honor and big deal to be a part of the dean's council, but when I met with the dean of the university, he said, 'Barbara, we're having a hard time getting women to join the council. We invite high-level women to come to the special dinner that we have and check us out and these women would pass on the offer almost every time.'

"So I went to one of those special dinners and I could immediately see why. And remember from earlier in our book, women will tell of a bad experience ten times more than men will. The dinner was a very old-school male-network drinking event. Some of the men were even 'flirting' with the women there, including me. I often froze. I had my hand kissed instead of shaken, which is what I was offering!"

YOU'RE CREATING A LOSE-LOSE SCENARIO

"Richard, we were also asked to look into the business schools and the actual content of the classes that they were delivering. And I sat in on one class in negotiations. The professor was one of the few tenured women professors at this top graduate school in the United States.

"She was so male in her behavior, yelling, 'Okay, everybody stop … stop!'

"She was actually shouting over the top of any discussions that were going on in that auditorium-style room. I thought to myself, what is she doing? We're having a dialogue here. The whole incident was over a negotiation game, and the game was all about winning the negotiation. Each team has a certain amount of money and they had to negotiate between each other.

"The team I was in was busy creating a win-win scenario, you know, you get this and we get that. And the professor said, 'Why would you want to lose? You're losing in that scenario.'

"One of the women on the team I was on was a top psychologist and asked the female professor, 'Have you read any of the studies on gender differences in negotiation?'

"The professor snapped back, 'No, why would I want to do that? We have a process here that we're following.'

"I then said, 'Yes, but right now, you're creating a lose-lose scenario. What you want is to get all the money. That's the name of the game.'"

"You know, Barbara, in my younger days, I remember it wasn't enough to win; the other guy had to lose. It is a sad commentary and an approach I learned was counter productive to long-term success."

"That's exactly right, Richard. The difference here was that there were six women around the table, all negotiating for a win-win, including a top woman leader from Lebanon, one from Ireland, and one from Geneva. And we're all negotiating this win-win and we all got zero scores from the professor!

"We left the session asking, 'Is that how we operate today? Is this what women are being taught in business schools? How to be a male when approaching business, in introducing ideas during meetings, or in negotiating?'"

FIXING THE PLUMBING

"I was watching an all-woman-hosted television show the other day where the guest was a male executive from one of the top television networks in the United States. He said, 'I think that the reason the women aren't advancing is that many just don't want it. They're much smarter than men for wanting a personal life, a whole life. And the top jobs are mostly filled with alpha male types who sacrifice a lot of personal things in life that women don't want to sacrifice.'

"I couldn't believe what I later discovered had happened shortly afterwards. That male executive speaking his mind was demoted for what he said. This is the exact thing *not* to do. In our work, we help men and women create congruency between intention and behavior, and his intention was to make a contribution. He was so engaged in the conversation and meant well, yet was penalized for saying the wrong thing. Women were so upset across the social media—the exact way *not* to feel or interpret his comments.

"The message is that we have to move away from the blame game, most especially blaming men for stepping in and engaging in the conversation. They shouldn't be penalized for saying the wrong thing, but instead engage in education and awareness building together. Create a win-win, not a win-lose. We need to stop that conversation."

"I couldn't agree more, Barbara, if we want to move more men from the 60 percent column, those who believe but don't know what to do—or what to say at times—to the column that are actively engaged, as this guy was trying to become, the blaming has to end."

"Richard, she could have said to him, 'You may have had the best of intentions in what you just said, but here's how it landed for me.' That kind of proactive conversation is what's needed today. We can solve anything if we can just communicate, drop our immediate defenses, and move beyond the blame game."

ENDNOTES

1. Danielle Gaucher, Justin Friesen, Aaron C. Kay, "Evidence That Gendered Wording in Job Advertisements Exists and Sustains Gender Inequality," *Journal of Personality and Social Psychology* 101, no. 1 (2011): 109–128, https://www.sussex.ac.uk/webteam/gateway/file.php?name=gendered-wording-in-job-adverts.pdf&site=7.
2. Ibid. p. 110.
3. Ibid. p. 111.
4. Jennifer Maki, CEO and executive director of Vale Canada, in a discussion with Barbara Annis, March 2016.

Chapter 11

WHAT THE FUTURE HOLDS

Throughout our book, we have shared statistics and stories of the ascent of women, now dominating education and moving into positions of leadership; we spoke of the ascent of men, in their recognition of and advocacy for women's leadership; and we highlighted the ascent of neuroscience and our expanding awareness of the distinct yet complementary natures of men and women.

We presented the business case and showed conclusively that women on boards and on executive teams improve an organization's innovativeness, decision making, productivity, and financial performance.

And we brought it all together with solutions to help you rid your company's "plumbing" of bias. We showed you where systemic biases can clog up the works and what gender-intelligent levers to pull in order to sustain an organization's gender diversity efforts and improve the intake, evaluation, promotion, and ultimate retention of its best talent.

> "Richard, we also shared stories of male leaders in all kinds of industries who get it, are championing the advancement of women, altering the cultures of their organizations, and positioning them for greater success.
>
> "I'd like to continue with recent stories of CEOs who had their enlightening moments, and through their leadership, took the steps to transform the culture of their companies and they themselves becoming active sponsors of advancing women in leadership. These men are of the 20 percent who get it and are doing something about it."

HOW ENGAGING ARE YOUR ENGAGEMENT SURVEYS?

While CEO of eBay from 2008 to 2015, John Donahoe and his executive team couldn't figure out why, after his immediate predecessor Meg Whitman left following ten years as CEO, there were significant retention issues with women not advancing and, instead, leaving the organization. It was confusing to the company since their periodic engagement surveys continued to indicate how there were no differences between the scores in how their male and female employees were viewing the company on work environment, learning opportunities, culture, and opportunities to advance.

His question to the team was, if men and women's engagement scores are more or less the same, why are we having trouble retaining women and sustaining gender diversity at the higher management levels?

Donahoe decided to dig deeper and engaged us to conduct a Gender Intelligence diagnostic with statements designed to uncover gender differences in attitudes and actions. Differences in men and women's attitudes began to emerge.

Employee responses at all levels of management indicated that diversity is valued at eBay; employees feel they can be heard; and that educational and networking opportunities are available. That's where the similarities ended and differences came to light in how women view their career and advance-ment opportunities. The women who took part in the Gender Intelligence diagnostic scored considerably *lower* than men on these statements:

- "There is an executive actively advocating for my career."
- "I have visibility into new job opportunities at eBay."
- "The most deserving people get promoted."
- "I feel free to make choices that give me the flexibility I need without hurting my career."
- "I get career advice from someone other than my manager when I need it."
- "If I had a daughter with the right skills and experience, I would encourage her to work here."

Interestingly, both women and men gave a higher score to the statement: "If I had a son with the right skills and experience, I would encourage him to work here." Unique questions such as these often reveal the hidden feelings of male and female employees on the deep-rooted culture of an organization.

Within a couple of weeks following the diagnostic, John Donahoe held a town hall meeting, webcasted across the global company, during which he stated his commitment to removing the challenges and obstacles to women's opportunity to advance at eBay.

He received a standing ovation that day that resonated for women and many men across the company in the weeks that followed. They had a male leader who not only got it, but was also actively involved in doing something about it. John Donahoe was getting to the underlying issues and actively engaged in changing the culture at eBay.

BRUSHING THE ENGAGEMENT SURVEY HORSE

"Barbara, remember my uncle's metaphor in Chapter 1 about brushing my horse? He said that I should go ahead and spend my time and effort on doing something that felt good to me. The fact that no one else (including my horse!) seemed to care didn't matter. It felt good to me. But remember, he also meant that I should not think just because I liked it and it felt good that anyone else would feel that way, or notice, or even care."

"Richard, the moral of your uncle's metaphor can be applied to engagement surveys. There's an enlightened denial in many companies when it comes to those studies. They're enlightened for wanting to poll their people and branding themselves as 'employee oriented' but in denial about how little value or meaning their surveys actually have to the people being polled.

"Let's definitely add non-dynamic engagement surveys to the list of what doesn't work.

"People typically are not riveted and involved when they're filling out employee engagement surveys. Companies ask the same questions year after year and it becomes nothing more than an annual routine with no significance and no outcome. Employees become numb to the questions or statements and will often jot down any response just to get through the survey. There's also apathy on the part of many women, some of whom just accept the fact that nothing will come of the survey. I've heard from women for whom engagement surveys feel insulting, as they basically ask, 'How's everything going?' but those surveyed never see any traction come from it.

"Leaders have told me that they've tried to get new questions or statements added to their surveys but often get pushback from the vendors who administer them. They seem to be more interested in using their surveys as a benchmarking mechanism. They can conduct their comparative analyses and sell that. And for the company, it becomes an 'already-budgeted-for' annual activity. Many leaders, though, are beginning to realize that netural or positive engagement survey results and declining retention rates, particularly for women, don't compute. Whether it be unseen systemic bias issues or the preferences and disposition of male leaders, something is missing, and it is often the commitment of the CEO."

"ARE WE BEING GENDER INTELLIGENT ABOUT THIS?"

My next male leader-as-example and a longtime champion of Gender Intelligence is the CEO of one of the largest financial services companies in the world. After attending a Gender Intelligence workshop along with his senior management team where we shared the business case and the science of gender differences, the CEO wanted to do everything he could to realize the extraordinary potential in the complement of the men and women on his senior team. He first declared that increasing the company's understanding of the value of gender differences in communication, problem solving, and decision making would take precedence at all levels of the organization and across all business units.

This was the first stage of awareness for the company, with leadership on down grasping the value of hardwiring and the advantage of Gender Intelligence. Within two years, it was commonplace during strategic planning sessions and team meetings throughout the company to hear men and women confirm the balanced thinking that went into their problem solving and decision making by checking themselves, asking, "Are we being gender intelligent about this?"

Today, all critical decisions at the executive level are made with the input of both men and women. Gender Intelligence even informs interactions with customers. By making this change, the company shifted its focus from identifying and reporting on the barriers to women's advancement to the innovative solutions rising out of a team able to take full advantage of its greater gender diversity and diversity in critical thinking skills.

CHALLENGING TRADITION

When Carlos Ghosn first took over as CEO of Nissan Motor Company in 1999, the company was on the verge of bankruptcy and drastic measures were called for to save the company. Ghosn took immediate and radically corrective measures at Nissan that challenged Japanese business etiquette, but produced results. Interestingly, though, it wasn't his closing of plants, cutting thousands of jobs, and spinning off the Nissan Aerospace division that offended Japanese cultural traditionalists.[1]

Research revealed that the clear majority of Nissan automobiles were bought either by women or because women heavily influenced the purchase decision. Clearly, women were Nissan's target market, yet there were *no* women in engineering, marketing, or sales at the company. Ghosn saw this as a huge gender blind spot. Nissan was underserving the needs and expectations of women purchasers by not involving women in the design phase, marketing, and selling of Nissan cars. He saw an opportunity for a marketplace breakthrough and accelerated growth by advancing women within Nissan.

Ghosn's first order of business was to create a shift in the mindsets of all Nissan employees to build greater awareness between men's and women's critical thinking skills and infuse Gender Intelligence in their actions and decisions. Employees learned how their differences could be used to improve the design and functionality of Nissan cars, create marketing campaigns that speak to women's needs and interests, and enhance selling strategies to better accommodate women's preferences for lower-pressure, high-transparency negotiation. Greater numbers of women were recruited and advanced within design, manufacturing, marketing, and sales.

As a result, Nissan realized a dramatic increase in sales and profitability. In 2008, it became the first company in Asia to win the Catalyst Award for gender diversity initiatives, which further served to attract the best women in engineering, marketing, and sales to the company.

FEMININE VALUES IN FINANCIAL SERVICES

Halla Tómasdóttir, cofounder of Audur Capital financial services, has been helpful in rebuilding Iceland's economy since its collapse in 2008. Her passion is releasing the incredible economic potential of women's ways of doing business.

Halla Tómasdóttir believes that women's values are key to solving Iceland's economic crisis. In 2007, Halla and her business partner, Kristin Pétursdóttir, cofounded Audur Capital to bring greater diversity, social responsibility, and "feminine values" to the financial services industry. These women-oriented values include independence, risk awareness, straight talk, emotional capital, and profit with principles. Audur's approach appears to be working and may just help save banking in Iceland.[2]

Research shows that in 2012, an index of sixty-seven hedge funds owned or managed by women in Iceland had a return of almost 9 percent, whereas an index that might be deemed more representative of the (male, white) industry generated 2.7 percent.[3]

Her simple conclusion is that, "More women are needed in finance, with this leading to less ego and more collaboration and more focus on emotional capital and less obsession with financial capital."[4]

At SunTrust we found many of the findings already in place as this story by CFO Aleem Gillani demonstrates:

> We (one male and one female) created, developed and implemented a new business strategy designed to generate a US$350M bottom-line benefit. Working together through carefully planned-out steps, the two of us collaborated on the development and implementation of a planning strategy.
>
> We partnered closely over the space of many months to carefully consider, fully analyze and confirm the merits of the strategy. We each took tasks aligned with our individual strengths. Looking back, I'd say this honest assessment of each of our strengths/weaknesses allowed for a much better approach and helped lead to ultimate success.
>
> When either of us encountered significant hurdles, we were supported and empowered by the other partner to refine, adjust or otherwise optimize the strategy. Given the sensitive and long-running nature of the project, as work progressed, we made sure to coach each other on executional aspects and appropriate messaging to all constituents.

The highly successful conclusion (which resulted in a nine figure net gain) has allowed both partners to obtain positive exposure throughout the company, our local community and our peers throughout the industry.[5]

—*Aleem Gillani*, CFO, SunTrust

WHY DOES GENDER SUCCESS ELUDE SO MANY BUSINESSES?

"Gender success" is a term used to describe the superior corporate performance that comes from men and women working together in balanced leadership, problem solving, and decision making.

Superior corporate performance refers to how the company performs relative to its peers in the same industry. Investors would like to own a company that generates superior performance. Bondholders would also appreciate it. Employees and job candidates seek out such companies. Governments appreciate the higher tax revenues that are generated. All of society benefits from greater innovation and a better environmental record. It seems clear that stakeholders want superior performance.

The evidence on how to generate superior performance has been known for the past decade. Adding women to boards and management improves corporate performance. The more diverse your company is, the better your performance will become.

Shareholders are directly involved in these issues. The evidence says that the company in which they own shares will perform better with a diverse management group of men and women. Then why do we not have that already? The answer must lie in the fact that companies are primarily run by men today and that men are largely comfortable with the situation as it exists. They either do not know the evidence that shows they could improve, or they do not believe it, or there is some countervailing force that causes them to discount the evidence in favor of the status quo. As we shared in Chapter 5, only 20 percent of men are in that category of "Don't get it and don't care to."

The problem is that a high percentage of that 20 percent of men are board members and senior executives—male leaders making the decisions. However, there are many male leaders, as you just read earlier and throughout this book, who do get it, are becoming involved, and changing the attitudes of other male leaders.

Once the preponderance of managers and directors (who happen today to be men) accept the evidence, the move to greater gender diversity will become a footrace to see who can get there first. We see the possible impact of adding more women to a board of directors. We know that adding women to the board will lead to more women on the top management team. This in turn will lead to more women throughout management. The starting point is for your company to accept the evidence around certain facts:

- Companies perform better if they include more women on their boards and in their management structure.
- Women and men are different. It is this difference, which we call gender diversity, which creates superior performance when they work together.

Many companies have adopted this strategy to achieve superior performance but the majority have not yet made this transition. This means there is substantial upside for those companies that do adopt this kind of approach.

WHAT IF WE DO NOT ACT?

There is a poem by Robert Frost that is learned by most schoolchildren, "The Road Not Taken," which ends as follow:

> Two roads diverged in a wood, and I—
> I took the one less traveled by,
> And that has made all the difference.[6]

We hope that *Results at the Top* has shown you ample evidence that adding gender diversity to your board and management teams will result in better performance. Yet this is the path that is still less travelled by most companies. If our companies continue to take the other road, the one that we stay on because we (men) are comfortable, they will fall behind other companies in the world that are going to be taking full advantage of the total employee population. The companies that do follow a gender-diverse path will gradually outperform companies that do not.

There are two especially troubling scenarios, which continue to raise the specter of a negative outcome. The positive outcome I have described in these pages is the one in which companies seek gender diversity because it is in their own interest to perform better. One negative scenario would be for future governments to declare that current slow process on diversity represents a form of market failure and they feel a need to act through quotas on gender composition of boards, management, and recruitment. Of course this would also entail regulatory oversight and reporting with sanctions applied for noncompliance.

If these strictures are applied only to public companies then, as in Norway, we may face the possibility of massive delisting from the stock exchange. This would be a backward step in the progress of better corporate governance. However, this is exactly what happened in Norway. Quotas come with many other negative consequences. Board members would never know whether they had been appointed to a board due to their competence or due to the quota system. This is unfair to all directors.

The costs of additional regulation including reporting and certification must be borne by someone. Either the corporate sector would be required to pick up the cost through fees or taxes, or the entire taxpayer base would be charged via higher taxes to pay these additional costs. In the quota scenario we will have successfully turned a positive outcome of gender diversity producing superior performance into a negative scenario of delisting, acrimony, loss of status, and higher costs.

The other negative scenario is one very few people have thought about. Some have mentioned this possibility to me but many will feel it is still in the category of the author going too far. Take the scenario of a company with the usual gender composition of a board with mostly men directors. Yes, they would have perhaps two female directors. The other fourteen would be men.

Now let's assume the company undertakes an acquisition. Over the next few years the acquisition does not perform as expected. In addition, divestitures that were supposed to happen have not happened due to weak performance not delivering the desired market price for these disposals.

Welcome to the nightmare scenario for companies and boards.

One day you come into the office to find out that shareholders have filed a class action lawsuit. The cause of action is inadequate gender diversity on the board. The lawsuit draws a direct connection between your poorly performing acquisition and inadequate due diligence by the board, inadequate discussion at the board level, the failure of most board members to ask questions about the proposed acquisition, and other reasons only lawyers can dream up.

The claimant in the lawsuit also wants damages for the company's failure to follow through on divestitures when the market was better disposed to accept these at a decent price. All of these failures are attributed to the gender composition of the board.

Boards establish their own gender composition by recommending a slate of directors to the shareholders. These directors are inevitably elected. However we know from the research presented in *Results at the Top* that women tend to ask more questions in board meetings, require more time in board sessions to discuss major decisions, and are more likely to follow through with asset sales. The board chose its composition and (so the shareholders' lawsuit alleges) this gender composition choice has damaged shareholders. Would the damages be for the company to pay, or would individual directors be held liable? A court would need to decide.

This scenario is pretty far-fetched, right? Wrong. In jurisdictions that have "comply or explain" regulations, the law requires companies and boards to achieve a certain standard set by regulators or provide reason(s) why you have not complied. Courts may see these standards as minimums any prudent company would follow if it were acting in the best interest of the corporation. If you comply with the minimum standards perhaps your company can argue that you followed regulatory instructions in your defense of the class action.

If you did not comply with the minimum standards you have accepted the risk of noncompliance. In the class action defense you will be at the mercy of the court, hoping that they accept your explanation for not complying with the minimum standard. This is similar to self-insurance. The company could have bought itself insurance by complying. Instead the company did not pay the cost of compliance, whatever that cost was, and now may be liable for the damages without any insurance.

Are these scenarios as low probability as past behavior by boards would indicate? It is impossible to tell given the pace of change. We have only had access for a few years to research relating to the impact of gender diversity on corporate performance. New regulations are only now coming into force. The impact of quotas is still being assessed. In this new world, which is still being formed, it may be more prudent to just get on with the job of fostering gender diversity in your firm. The following section discusses major actions that can be taken by companies to put them on this less traveled road.

STEPS TO GENDER SUCCESS

We start with a quotation from a CEO of a banking group:

> The cultural aspects of a company are very important and you have to drive an organization toward those behaviors that you want. So, one, you have to state exactly what you expect—what good looks like. Two, you have to get people in place that model that behavior. And, three, you have to value behaviors—how you value the result as much as the result itself.[7]

This CEO is definitely headed in the right direction. Publicly undertaking a strategy, establishing role models, and setting rewards for desired results are normal techniques used by experienced managers. In the case of gender success they are only part of what is required. Change at this societal level is tough and will take a truly committed effort. We know it is possible as a few firms are already doing it and reaping the results.

Here are the actions that *Results at the Top* has shown will improve a company's performance through gender-diverse leadership and governance.

1. Public Support of Diversity

The CEO and top management adopt a publicly visible, supportive, and comprehensive statement regarding the company's approach to diversity at all levels within the organization.

This expectation must be permeated through all levels of the company. It must be repeated regularly.

2. Fix the "Plumbing"

As we delineated in Chapter 10, ensure that the "plumbing" of the company has eliminated systemic bias. "Plumbing" refers to the processes within the company that affect the intake, evaluation, promotion, and ultimate retention of employees. Look for the following:

- **Systemic bias in benefits programs.** Human resource department should examine all policies under the direction of the gender diversity officer (see point 4).
- **Uncompetitive or unacceptable maternity leave benefits and practices.** Assign a different manager to be responsible for the retention of each professional maternity leave employee. This manager is to be in regular contact with the employee and to assist them in reintegration back into the firm. This will be part of the manager's evaluation for the period.
- **Incorrect mandate and lopsided gender composition of graduate intake teams.** Closely examine the actions of these teams to ensure they are consistent with an unbiased approach to intake. Look at their actions with potential employees, their recruitment materials, and how they conduct themselves in actual interactions.
- **New hires from both outside the firm and promotions to new roles within the firm must formally document the candidates considered, including by gender.** Searches that do not involve acceptable levels of diversity should be rejected and completed again.
- **Broaden the source of new graduates and other new employees** to include other disciplines and other geographies looking for new employees who have a record of achievement and effort.
- **Incorrect mandate and lopsided gender composition of promotion committees.** Top management should examine the promotion committee procedures, recommendations, and their record of the type of promotions they have recommended in the past. Additional information should be examined on how well past-promoted employees have performed.
- **Conduct of management must show the appropriate respect for all employees.** Ongoing training of management is needed to ensure that unintentional or intentional bias is recognized and eliminated from the conduct of managers.
- **Celebrate role models on a gender-diverse basis.** Make certain role models exist for all to see, both men and women.
- **Succession planning** must be conducted in a gender-diverse environment and with expectation that candidates will be gender diverse.

3. Board of Directors to Achieve Gender Balance

The board of directors should adopt a gender-diverse composition that is balanced within a reasonable time. We use the word "balance" here because boards themselves can choose how they achieve this composition. Is the board balanced fifty-fifty between women and men? Research presented in this book indicates that increasing benefits will accrue to companies up to the point at which parity is reached.

As long as boards receive benefit from diversity they should continue to seek those benefits by increasing diversity. New board candidates should be sought from a wider cross section of society. This will produce benefits in the governance of the company as well as set a role model for senior management that will lead to more women top managers. In this context, it is particularly important to ensure that board committee chairs are diverse.

4. Appoint a Gender Diversity Officer with Real Power

Appoint a very senior individual as the gender diversity officer and provide them with the power and resources to change the company. This person could be a man or woman as long as they have a record of success in getting the job done. They should report directly to the CEO and should not be part of the human resources department of the firm. Over time, as the firm achieves its targets, the position may change or disappear completely but this should not happen until targets are achieved and there is confidence that Gender Success will be maintained.

5. Measure Company Performance and Take Action Where Needed

Companies should create a comprehensive gender-diversity management information system. The Gender Propensity Index© proposed in Chapter 9 of this book should be viewed as a starting point. Companies should use this type of measurement system to determine their relative performance compared to other firms over time. Stakeholders will use this information for a variety of purposes.

6. Publicly Report Progress at All Levels

Publicly report your progress on gender diversity at all levels of the management structure. Companies need to measure their performance at all management levels and to introduce strategies to prevent systemic bias in employee hiring, the existence of glass ceilings, and the attrition of women employees.

THE LONG ASCENT

Throughout this book we have observed that it is up to men to work with women to achieve this improvement in the way we run our businesses. It is up to men to consent to the addition of more women on boards and on management teams. Why should they give this consent? They should simply because their companies will perform better. The business case is clear and the time when we now need more qualified leaders is today.

Imagine how different our world would be right now if women had been at the table just in the last fifty years. The solution, right under our noses, is in bringing the best brains of men and women together to create a better, more stable world—both economically and socially.

We firmly believe that gender diversity and the advancement of women in leadership will experience tremendous gains and the solution is by engaging men to be a part of the movement.

This entire book has underscored the role models of women in leadership and the role models of men in support whose advocacy is making a difference. They are the evidence of change and what the future can hold where men and women share leadership.

The next ten years will show tremendous progress for gender diversity. We're on the crest and beginning to see the effects of that gender-balanced leadership on the productivity and financial performance of companies. That crest will carry over onto the global economy and in governments across the globe.

Aside from women's growing numbers in business, we're seeing more and more female leaders emerge as presidents and prime ministers, as senators and members of parliament, contributing their own authentic expression of power and leadership. We've had strong women leaders in government before. Yet, in many instances, their leadership echoed traditional male leadership traits.

We believe the engagement of women in developing countries for their balanced voice in business and government has the potential to solve their countries' issues as well as bring countries together to solve global issues to break the impasse on seemingly endless disagreements, encourage deeper and more meaningful dialogue, and forestall violent conflicts and wars.

"Richard, the situation is continuing to evolve forward as gender differences in leadership and governance are showing the way for the next generation of women and men in leadership—women expressing their own authentic voice alongside that of men."

"Barbara, I'd like to speed up that evolution and I know you would too. Our message to men is a simple one. You *have* to do this! It's clearly in your interest and in the interests of your organizations. Do it now!"

ENDNOTES

1. Bill Snyder, "Carlos Ghosn: Five Percent of the Challenge Is the Strategy. Ninety-Five Percent Is the Execution," *Stanford Business*, July 9, 2014, https://www.gsb.stanford.edu/insights/carlos-ghosn-five-percent-challenge-strategy-ninety-five-percent-execution.

2. Una McCaffrey, "Icelandic 'Sister' Who Believes in the Power of Women in Finance," *Irish Times*, March 2, 2015, http://www.irishtimes.com/business/work/icelandic-sister-who-believes-in-the-power-of-women-in-finance-1.2120468.

3. Ibid.

4. Ibid.

5. Aleem Gillani, CFO, Suntrust, in an interview with Richard Nesbitt, August 2016.

6. Robert Frost, "The Road Less Traveled" (originally published 1916), Poetry Foundation, https://www.poetryfoundation.org/resources/learning/core-poems /detail/44272.

7. Georges Desvaux and Sandrine Devillard, "Women Matter 2013—Gender Diversity in Top Management: Moving Corporate Culture, Moving Boundaries," McKinsey and Company, 2013: 15.

INDEX

171